"More Retail Details...
Mother Forgot to Mention"

Another Small Store Survival Guide & Reference Book
For Gift & Apparel Retailers

By T.J. Reid

Retail Resources Publications
P.O. Box 977
Amite, Louisiana 70422
800-221-8615
www.tjreid.com

<u>More</u> Retail Details ... *Mother Forgot to Mention*
Another Small Store Survival Guide & Reference Book
For Gift & Apparel Retailers

Published by:
Retail Resources Publications
P.O. Box 977
Amite, Louisiana 70422

800-221-8615
504-748-8930 fax
www.tjreid.com

Limits of Liability and Disclaimer of Warranty
The author and publisher shall not be liable in the event of incidental or consequential damages in connection with, or arising out of, the furnishing, performance, or use of instructions and/or claims of productivity gains. The author and publisher make no warranty of any kind, expressed or implied, with regard to the instructions and suggestions contained within.

FIRST EDITION
Copyright 1999 by T.J. Reid
First Printing 1999
Printed in the United States of America
10 9 8 7 6 5 4 3 2 1

ISBN 1-880522-25-X

Book cover design by Graphix Plus
Some illustrations by Brian Chaffin
Editorial assistant: Laura Lea Reid

Foreword from ☆T.J.

When I wrote "What Mother Never Told Ya About Retail" several years ago, I thought I I had included everything there was to know about owning and managing a small retail specialty shop. After all, I had successfully handled the job for over twenty years, winning awards and making profits! What else was there to know? A lot - I soon began to realize.

As more and more retailers and would-be store owners purchased the book, the more phone calls I received. Each one was very complimentary concerning the book and it's guidance, but then there would be that "Can I ask you a couple of things?" Immediately, I would think "Why didn't I mention that?" Or "How could I leave out something that important?"

So I set out to learn more to assist those starting out fresh, as well as those who had been around for years, and were still struggling to make a success of their small specialty stores. My second book, "52 Promotions - A Year's Worth of Profit!", tried to fill in the advertising and promotional gaps by including many of the outstanding examples sent in by small store owners from across the nation. Still, there were so many additional topics dealing with specialty retailing that I had left out of the original survival guide; I immediately began work on the follow-up edition you are now reading.

Since it all begins with a product to sell, this starts with the basics of going to market and placing orders. It may sound elementary to a seasoned veteran, but every day I run into store owners who have been around for fifteen or twenty years, and still don't use any type of classifications to track their inventory. Most retailers don't use their own order forms at market; many don't know their markup percentages; some can't figure their profit margins. Yesterday I received a phone call from a lady who was about to celebrate her 25th anniversary; she was asking how to figure an open-to-buy. See, it's never too late to learn.

Networking with retailers at market centers, trade shows and over the phone I am constantly discovering new and better ways to profit in this business. I look and listen and marvel at the talents of today's store owners. The sample employee handbook included in this book came from The Antique Boutique, a wonderful family-owned business in south Texas. The promotional hints from Hendersons, come from a third-generation department store which is the anchor of their small downtown Illinois retail environment. Debbie Allen, owner of Ap'ropo in Arizona divides her time between managing her successful store, and pursuing a career in speaking and consulting; she added suggestions you'll see in the Image section. My friend, Libby of Jon Marc from a small North Carolina community is mentioned in later chapters also. Our close personal friendship and our decade old business relationship have been a wonderful learning and sharing experience.

As I visit and work with these retailers in so many varied parts of the country, I feel as if I take a little piece of each one with me when I leave. Every store has their own special way of working with customers and establishing their own unique place in their community. So many retailers like Carol Jo, Dee, Kathryn, Marion, Marilyn . . . not just store owners, but friends and comrades in this wonderful business I love, have influenced my life and the advice given in this new book. Without them and others like them, there would be no book, and no retail story to continue.

> This book is dedicated to all those hardworking, wonderful, creative mavens who share their love and talents with me and retailers everywhere . . . Read, react and respond!

3

SPECIAL CONTRIBUTORS: *Words from the Wise*

Although I wanted this to be <u>my</u> sequel to ***"What Mother Never Told Ya About Retail*,"** one of the first things I realized after writing that book was *"You never stop learning."* I have made so many friends in the retail speaking, writing, and consulting field, and each one of these people have been a tremendous asset to my life and my business education.

I am so happy to be able to share some of their knowledge with you by including some of their wise words, covering many phrases of retail. These people are very respected in the industry and known for their expertise in retail business. I whole heartedly recommend their services and their advice.

☆**Debbie Allen** - "The Retail Motivator" of Image Dynamics, an award winning women's specialty store owner and retail speaker, author and consultant. She can be reached at 800-359-4544, fax 602-948-7487 or by e-mail at dallen7001@aol.com

☆**Margie Johnson** of Shop Talk, a firm which provides comprehensive services in consultation, management and market research to hundreds of clients nationwide. An acclaimed speaker, trainer and consultant with a wonderful reputation, and almost thirty years of experience, she can be reached at 757-491-1411, fax 757-491-1311 or e-mail Shoptalk@ix.netcom.com

☆**Sally McDevitt** of Retail Fashion Right, a firm specializing in retail buyer training and crew training, can be reached at 972-540-5634, e-mail sallymcde@aol.com.

☆**Bob Nelson** of Power Retailing is a marketing genius with "the power to take your sales to the top." The phone number is 602-460-1980, fax 602-460-1981, e-mail is bnelson@retailing.com. I suggest you visit his award-winning website www.retailing.com. It is wonderful!

☆**Lynne Schwabe**, a speaker, trainer, author, consultant and star of many videos on retail is also one of America's visual merchandising authorities. A regular contributor to FASHION ADVANTAGE for almost a decade, she can be reached 540-687-3876, fax 540-687-3131.

☆**Rick Segel** of Rick Segel & Associates is one of my dearest and oldest friends in the industry, dating back to our days as retailers, and members of the same buying group. A seasoned retailer, he has authored books, and audio and video programs on retail. He is a retail trainer, consultant, and truly one of the best speakers I have ever heard. Phone 781-272-9995, fax 781-272-9996, and e-mail RSegel@aol.com.

Table of Contents

Enjoy . . . I think you're gonna ❤ it!

So You Want To Open A Store?

There are so many things to think about: finances, locations, leases, licenses, employees, display, advertising, market trips, image. I have tried to cover each and every topic in the following pages, even down to comparing malls to free-standing buildings. I've included employee handbook samples, your own order copy samples, and a list of what to take to take to market.

As I was finishing the book I realized I had not discussed floor plans for your new store, but then that will depend greatly on what kind of business you are undertaking: gift or apparel? Here are some of interior problems you'll need to deal with in the initial planning stages.

<u>Important factors to consider</u>:

✓ Where will the register check-out island be placed?

✓ What about the gift wrap area?

✓ How many phone jacks and where? Same for electrical outlets. There are never enough in the right places.

✓ What style fixtures? What is the store logo and image?

✓ How much space for an office? Will it be private enough for business conversations and staff discussions?

✓ Where is the stockroom? Is it large enough? Near the selling floor?

✓ Will there be customer restrooms? (YES!)

Your first financial step is to register your new business as required in the city, the county and the state, and with the federal government for a sales tax license and employer's tax I.D.

Determine if you wish to be a sole owner, a partnership, a corporation, etc. There are advantages and troubles with each, so weigh carefully your options with the assistance of a CPA or your bank representative.

More friendships are destroyed through joint business ventures than lover's quarrels. I suggest you give a great deal of thought *(and prayer)* before losing a dear friend and a fortune in a "retail friendship fantasy store partnership." If you want to operate a business - great - go for it! If you just want to have a good time together - go shopping at retail, it's cheaper!

To Market - To Market

Your first market trip is always an exciting experience. Plan to spend enough time to see everything you want to order, as well as acquaint yourself with the market areas. Even the most seasoned buyer sometimes likes to spend the first day of a market *"just looking"* around. It is a good way to get your bearings and get a feel for the latest trends. As you stroll the aisles of a booth show or check out the showrooms in a market setting, just jot down the names and numbers of lines that look interesting. Prepare the list in order, either by merchandise category or building location, and then begin to work.

I personally always liked to do lines by category. It seemed easier to compare sweaters to sweaters and dresses to dresses that way. I would allot time for sportswear, dresses, jeans, etc. and then do my accessories last, using the previous order copies to make sure I was buying things that would accent and co-ordinate. Gifts I worked by market floors and line locations. They are such an impulse buy that I constantly saw something here or there and couldn't resist. I found it very difficult to take booth numbers and return, so I just wrote orders as I found what I liked. (It worked!)

First things first... let's talk about what you need to bring to market with you. On your first trip, call the market you plan to attend and check for their admission requirement qualifications. Each one is different, but most require a business card, a picture I.D., your resale tax permit and a void business check. For additional employee registration, a canceled payroll check and business card are needed for each person. After you are on their permanent list, it becomes much simpler. You can usually register in advance, and have your badge waiting for pickup at the front desk.

If you are seeking to buy with a line of credit (aren't we all?), it will be necessary that you have financial statements (one for every company you place an order with, bring extras). For first time buying, a letter of credit or introduction from your bank is also helpful.

During the day you will pick up catalogs, pamphlets, order forms and on occasion - free gifts from sales reps and company showrooms. Be prepared by carrying a large shoulder bag or backpack. Many buyers like those little roll-along bags with wheels that are easy to navigate through the hallways. In your bag, you will need business cards, a calculator, cash for vending machines and food court, an extra pair of hosiery (you know you're gonna run 'em), freshen-up cosmetics, and a rubber stamp. (You will thank me over and over for this suggestion.)

A rubber stamp will make filling out forms so fast and easy. You can register in showrooms, place orders, get on mailing lists - everything just by stamping! On the stamp you should have: Business name, business address, business phone, business fax, and e-mail address.

I had my own order copies printed, and preferred to always use them when placing orders. You will find a lot of vendors will not like this, but it is your money and for your convenience, so insist. If they offer preprinted forms - especially those with sketches, take a full set of copies so you can file them with your own order forms for later reference and re-order. By using your own order forms which are the same size, color and shape, you are able to file them neatly in your own binder system. (A sample order form has been included on page 10; you can design your own to meet your individual store needs and inventory systems.)

Needless to say, I am assuming you have arrived at market with an open-to-buy plan and a budget for the coming season, as well as immediate goods. If not - stay home. You'll be better off financially and emotionally down the line.

Your friends at home, your employees, and especially your spouse, always assume that you are having a great party time at market. For some unfounded reason, they act like you have taken a long relaxing vacation. How little they know and understand. Market usually means tired feet, an aching back, and headaches. Here are a few of my survival tactics for making market trips enjoyable:

Arrive with your budget and open-to-buy in hand, and major appointments already scheduled. This will enable you to get a good nights sleep prior to that first big day. Schedule appointments so that you have free time in between to just look around or even catch a short 20 minute afternoon nap. Don't dare try to do the 7 to 7 routine, and *then* hit the local wholesales after dark. Spend enough time in town to get all your work done without collapsing from overwork and exhaustion.

Be comfortable - you're not the fashion show. That said, I realize you aren't going to follow that rule. It's market and everyone likes to show off their latest looks. OK, just at least remember to wear *old* comfortable shoes. Nothing feels worse at market than a brand new pair of shoes!

Limit your alcohol and food intake. This is a time for business; you need a clear head and a fresh body to get all this work done. In the evening, work on orders in your room or network with other store owners who share your same interests. It'll be a profitable evening, and they'll understand your early bedtime departure. Rest is essential!

Occasionally bring an employee or friend to market with you. You will enjoy having someone to share opinions, and carry the briefcase. This can be an excellent way to reward a deserving employee. (They will think it is fun - not work, at least on the first day or so.)

Regarding wardrobe - call ahead the day before you leave for market. I have been caught in snow storms in Dallas in March, and have frozen in Denver in August. There is nothing worse than being forced to buy extra clothes *(at retail)* to survive market.

After determining your wardrobe needs for the climate, don't overpack. Leave plenty of room in your suitcase for those special items you're bound to come across. No buyer ever leaves market without purchasing personals, those all-important employee gifts, sample finds, and the list goes on. Who can resist, it *is* wholesale.

If you go overboard at market, there is always the availability of shipping things home by UPS or Fed Ex, but don't let those order copies out of your sight. I once packed my incomplete orders, market notes and order copies in my checked luggage. When it was lost, my entire market trip was destroyed. Those are items which you should always hand carry. Actually. I suggest that buyers take the time to complete and add all their orders before leaving market. Turn them in before you leave town and your trip home will be much more relaxing.

Put a smile on your face! Your own attitude towards life is what determines how life treats you. Network with as many store owners as possible. Start conversations on the shuttle bus, in the hotel lobby, in showrooms, and elevators. Collect as many business cards as possible. Share your love and excitement for this industry.

I love seeing store owners wearing those rhinestone pins that read "BUSINESS IS GREAT!" My daughter believes in the theory, *"Everything we say either creates or destroys."* If you come to market griping and complaining about the economy, the customers, the salesmen, the weather - it will all probably remain the same because you are continuing to destroy with your negative thoughts and actions. Instead, arrive at market prepared with a professional and enthusiastic attitude to create a profitable season.

Writing An Order for Merchandise
How It All Begins

There is such a thrill when you sign your name to the bottom of that first order copy. I still remember back thirty years: it was a company named Thermo-Jac; the sales rep was Harold "Bunny" Bridges and the total was $350.00! (It's sort of like your first kiss, if you truly love it - you don't forget. It's filed away in your life's precious memory bank.)

On the following page I show a sample order form which I used at market. This form was made in triplicate so the top copy went to the company sales representative for the manufacturer, the second was for my order files and the third was used by our receiving department to check in goods. This is also a convenient form to use later when determining the selling ratio of items.

When placing an order on your own paper (order form) you will need the complete company information including address, phone, fax, and customer service department contact. I found that you will spend more time discussing your problems with this person than your sales representative, although you do need the identical information on file for the sales office also.

Checklist of necessary information:

✓ Date the order is placed
✓ Beginning delivery and completion date
✓ Quantities, sizes and colors
✓ Means of transportation (UPS, USPO, Fed Exp or cheapest way)
✓ Cost per item
✓ Payment terms (8/10, EOM, C.O.D., etc.)
✓ TOTAL OF ORDER

Never turn in an incomplete, untotaled or unsigned order form. Almost every sales representative is an honest person . . . but, don't take any chances with your money. You can easily be deceived. What appears to be just a few pieces may total out more than your budget allows. It is much easier to not order, than to be forced to cancel. Take this precaution now - not later, and your relationship with the company and the sales representative will remain friendly.

There is the age old question: *"Should I turn my orders in when I write them in the showroom?"* And there is the age old debate over that answer. There are several reasons why I suggest that you turn your orders in before leaving market:

✓ You have had time to shop and compare; your decision should be made.
✓ You have the orders totaled and your budget calculated.
✓ The information is fresh in your mind so you can make clear decisions.
✓ By taking orders home you take the risk of losing delivery date.
✓ By taking orders home, you can easily forget what you saw, not understand your notes and end up with things you do not want or even like.

As you can see from the above paragraph, I don't necessarily believe you have to turn the order in while in the showroom, but I do *recommend strongly* that all orders are left at market with the vendors.

Store Name
Address
Phone and Fax Number

Purchase Order #: _____

Manufacturer: _____

Address: _____

Phone Number: _____

Contact: _____

Bill to: _____

Ship to: _____

Order date: _____	**Terms:** _____
Start date: _____	**When to ship:** _____
Complete date: _____	**Cancel if not shipped by:** _____

Style #	Description	Color	Quantity	Line Price	Unit Price	Receipt Date

Merchandise shipped and invoices dated on or after the 20th of the month should be billed to us as of the 1st of the following month. All 10-day datings begin at the date of receipt of shipment by us. The seller hereby agrees to protect us against all claims and damage for infringements or copyrights in acceptance of this order. Vendor agrees to furnish a guarantee that all textile fiber products specified are herein labeled in accordance with the Federal Fiber Textile Products Indentification Act. Permanent care labeling regulations are in compliance with all other federal and state laws.

Authorized by: _____

Date: _____

How-To Get The Most Out of A Seminar

At markets I frequently see some of the same people over and over in a seminar audience. Ironically, these are usually also the most successful people in their perspective areas. Why then do they continue to repeatedly attend workshops and seminars concerning what they are already doing so well?

Because of the theory, *"It's what you learn after you know it all that really counts!"* And it's so very true. These successful people have learned life's greatest lesson - you never stop learning. After repeatedly doing the same task over and over again, it becomes bland, unexciting. Retailers need to attend seminars to pick up new ideas and put the thrill back in their job. Or as Stella would say, *"To get their groove back."*

Successful seminars depend largely upon the attitude and participation of every member. Arrive with a clear mind, ready to learn, and you will take home new ideas to implement into your store system.

To make any learning experience beneficial you should:

▼ Realize the seminars belong to you. Markets plan these with the buyers interest in mind. Sessions are to help you in managing your retail business.

▼ Recognize the success of the seminar rests partly with you and your attitude and desire to learn. Don't arrive with a *"I know it all"* attitude. You are here to learn and if you allow yourself, you will take at least one or two good ideas home from each session you attend.

▼ Enter into the discussion enthusiastically. Take part in the networking. Give your opinion, and share ideas that have worked for you. This is give and take - not just taking. Bring business cards to pass out to those you wish to stay in contact with.

▼ Confine your discussion to the topic at hand.

▼ Only one person should talk at a time. Avoid private conversations while someone is speaking. No one ever learned anything with their mouth open.

▼ Listen alertly to the discussions.

▼ Arrive on time prepared; do not slip out before the completion.

▼ Ask questions to be certain you understand what the speaker has said.

▼ Take brochures and handouts home for further review or to contact the speaker later.

▼ Complete seminar evaluation forms to aide in planning next seminar topics, times, dates, etc. The market staff which plans seminar events depends on the advice and evaluation of attendees. Unless you tell them what you want, they have no way of knowing. Offer suggestions on topics, speakers, times, days. This will make the education director's job much easier and insure that you get a program that you want and can enjoy.

Apparel Marts Nationwide

The major fashion center of the United States has always been considered New York City. It is true that five days a week, 52 weeks a year, you can go into New York and find all the merchandise you could ever need to run your clothing stores, but I have always believed small-to-medium specialty stores can do better by attending their regional shows on a regular basis, and special events such as the International Boutique Show, the Fashion Accessories Expo, and WWD Magic once a year. New York, like every regional fashion center, has five major fashion market each year and those dates vary from year to year.

The majority of specialty owners feel lost in the New York buying environment, without a buying office. (Even accompanied by a buyer, I felt uncomfortable.) There are too many buildings, too many lines, and too many showrooms to choose from spread out throughout the garment district. An important consideration: the cost of travel to New York is sometimes as much as double that of other cities where regional markets are located. In my opinion, the major drawback to shopping the New York market is not working with your area sales representative. In each area of the country fashion trends vary, as do fabric choices. What is flying off the racks in Minneapolis may be on the markdown rack in Georgia. While Texas girls always love big earrings and longer prairie skirts, a New York rep may want to sell the minimalist look and mini skirts. The company representative for your region will be able to better assist you in selecting styles for your particular climate and customer base. (Refer to your Bureau of Wholesale Representatives pages 124-127 to locate the group showing in your area.)

I have been a featured speaker at every apparel and gift market center in the country, and am proud to list and recommend the following regional market centers:

ATLANTA

AmericasMart Apparel
250 Spring Street, NW
Atlanta, Georgia 30303
(404) 220-3000 phone
(404) 220-2813 fax
(888) AMC - FAX1 (Fax on demand)
(800) 241-6405 Travel Discount Information
(800) APPAREL is Buyer Information
(877) LINELIST (Looking for lines)
E-Mail: pmorton@americasmart.com
Website: http://www.americasmart.com
Executive Director of Mart Relations is Milton Crane
Director of Marketing is Pam Morton
Marketing Manager is Dana Smith

Atlanta features more than 1,000 showrooms of women's, children's and men's apparel, plus accessories. Located in downtown Atlanta, it is 15 minutes from Hartsfield Airport, and is within walking distance of numerous hotels.

CHARLOTTE

Charlotte Apparel Center
2500 East Independence Blvd.
Charlotte, N.C. 28205
(704) 376-3006
(704) 376-2833 fax
(800) 763-4727 is Buyer Information
Director is Mike Realon, Extension #102
The I.F.M.A. headquarters is in Charlotte Mart.
The Charlotte Apparel Mart has 100 permanent showrooms.
The Charlotte Apparel Center is located 5 miles from the Charlotte Douglas Airport.

CHICAGO

Chicago Apparel Center
350 North Orleans Street
Chicago, Il. 60654
(800) 677-6278
(312) 527-4141
(312) 527-7971 fax
(800) 528-8799 For Mart Center Travel
website:www.merchandisemart.com
Director of Marketing is Christy Young

The Chicago Apparel Center is located 30 minutes from Chicago O'Hare Airport and about 40 minutes from Chicago Midway. It is within walking distance of several downtown hotels and adjoins the Holiday Inn Mart Plaza, Chicago.

DALLAS

Dallas Apparel Mart
2300 Stemmons Freeway
Dallas, Texas 75258
(214)655-6100
(214) 638-7221 fax
(800) DAL-MKTS information
(800)325-6587 Buyer Information
(800) 637-6833 Fax on Demand
E-mail: dmc@dallasmarketcenter.com
Website: http.www.dallasmarketcnter.com
Director of Retail Relations is Kimberly Wise
Label Link Service - (800) DAL-MKTS
The Dallas Apparel Mart is made up of over 1,000 showrooms featuring men's, women's' and children's apparel, plus accessories. It is located 25 minutes from the Dallas Fort-Worth Airport and 10 minutes from Love Field.

DENVER

Denver Apparel Mart
451 East 58th Avenue
Denver, Colorado 80216
(303) 292-6278
(303) 298-1503 fax
(800) BUY-MART Buyer Information
Director of Buyer Services is Karen Woods

The Denver Apparel Market is about 35 minutes from Denver International Airport and adjoins the Quality Inn Hotel North at the Mart (303-297-1717).

KANSAS CITY

Kansas City Apparel Mart
1775 Universal Avenue #1650
Kansas City, Missouri 64120
(816) 231-6446
(816) 231-4703 Fax
Show Co-ordinator is Alisa McConnell

The Kansas Apparel Market is located 40 minutes from Kansas City International and features 15 permanent showrooms as well as temporary show facilities five times a year. The Park Place Hotel (1-800-821-8532) is within walking distance of the center.

LOS ANGELES

California Apparel Mart
110 East Ninth Street
Los Angeles, California 90070
(213) 630-3600
(213) 630-3780 fax
(800) 225-6278
(800) 404-0244 Fax on Demand
Website: http://www.californiamart.com
Marketing Director is Susan Hicks

The Cal-Mart is located in downtown Los Angeles, approximately 30 minutes from Los Angeles International Airport.

MIAMI

Miami Apparel Mart
777 NW 72nd Avenue
Miami, Florida 33126
(305) 261-2900
(305) 261-3659 fax
Website: http.//www.mimm.com

Miami International Merchandise Mart has 220 showrooms which carry men's, women's and children's apparel and accessories. It is located 3 miles from Miami International Airport.

MINNEAPOLIS

Minneapolis Apparel Market
1300 Nicolette Mall #4052
Minneapolis, Minnesota 55403
(612) 333-5219
(612) 333-5226 fax
(800) 272-6972 Buyer Information
Show Manager is Joan Peterson
Co-ordinator is Nancy Goetzman

The Minneapolis Apparel Market is located 18 miles from Minneapolis International Airport. The market center has fifty showrooms featuring women's, children's and men's apparel plus accessories.

Important Travel Numbers

Most market centers and trade shows have travel departments which will gladly handle your advance reservations for you. Just in case you get in a bind or want to tackle the job alone, here are all the numbers you could possibly need.

AIRLINES:

American Airlines	1-800-433-7300
American West	1-800-235-9292
Delta	1-800-221-1212
Frontier Airlines	1-800-432-1359
Midwest Express	1-800-452-2022
Northwest Airlines	1-800-225-2525
Southwest Airlines	1-800-I FLY SWA
TWA	1-800-221-2000
United Airlines	1-800-241-6522
US AIR	1-800-428-4322
ValuJet	1-800-825-8538
Virgin Atlantic	1-800-862-8621

MAJOR HOTELS:

Best Western Worldwide	1-800-528-1234
Budget Host Inns	1-800-BUD HOST
Days Inn of America	1-800-Day INNS
Doubletree Hotels	1-800-222-TREE
Embassy Suites	1-800-EMBASSY
Hampton Inns	1-800-HAMPTON
Hilton Hotels	1-800-HILTONS
Holiday Inns	1-800-HOLIDAY
Howard Johnson	1-800-I GO HOJO
Hyatt Hotels	1-800-233-1234
ITT Sheraton	1-800-325-3535
Marriott Hotels & Suites	1-800-228-9290
Radisson Hotels	1-800-333-3333
Ramada Inns & Limiteds	1-800-2 RAMADA
Red Roof Inns	1-800-471-3735
Ritz Carlton	1-800-241-3333
Westin Hotels	1-800-228-3000
Wyndham	1-800-WYNDHAM

Trade Shows Held Nationwide
GIFT & APPAREL

When seeking information on apparel shows held at permanent apparel marts nationwide, contact those listed in that section. When seeking information about regional apparel shows, the information can be found on the Bureau of Wholesale Representatives show list. The following list is a combination of every single show I could locate across the country - that is *not* in an apparel market or a bureau show.

This list includes fashion, accessories, display materials, gift, souvenir, home furnishings, crafts and a little bit of everything thrown in. If you need any of these products, they should be at one of these shows. Please call for show dates and location. Then always reconfirm before making definite travel plans. Show dates do often change.

After you attend several shows and subscribe to trade magazines, you will find yourself on every show's mailing list. For now, just call the ones that interest you for additional information. Every show has a phone listing, and those that have permanent facilities, also have location. If it is listed as nationwide, the same group shows several places throughout the country. In many cases, the same trade show company may be the reference for several different categories of shows. When speaking with a contact person, ask if they sponsor other shows that might interest you and be appropriate for your business.

A- STYLE - Javits Center - New York...212-741-3653

Accessorie Circuit - Piers 92 & 94 - New York.................................212-759-8055

Action Sports Retailer Trade Expo - nationwide..............................714-376-8144

Activewear Show - nationwide...407-842-4100

ACC Craft Fair - Many locations around the country.......................914-883-6100

Asia Fashion Fair - Hong Kong...212-615-2850

Atlanta Gift & Merchandise Show...404-220-2204

Atlanta International Western & English Show.................................800-742-3184

Atlantic City Variety Show - New Jersey...800-950-1314

Atlantic City Trade Show - New Jersey...800-421-4511

Beckman Handcrafted Gift Shows - nationwide................................323-962-5424

BIG & TALL Women's Show - Las Vegas..305-663-6635

Book Expo of America - Chicago, Il...203-840-5460

Boston Gift Show - Bayside Center - Boston....................................914-421-3200

Boston Center Gift Show..800-435-2775

Buyers Market of American Crafts - nationwide...............................410-889-2933

CC Craft Fair - Nationwide...914-883-6100

California Gift Show - L.A. Convention Center.......................213-362-5640

Canadian Gift & Tableware Show - throughout Canada....................416-679-0170

Catalog in Motion - Tucson, Az...800-396-9896

Charlotte Gift Mart - Charlotte, N. C...................................704-377-5881

Chicago Gift Show - McCormack Place - Chicago, Il....................914-421-3200

Chicago Gift & Merchandise Show -Mart - Chicago, Il...................800-677-MART

Columbus Ohio Gift Show..614-876-2719

Dallas Gift & Merchandise Market...214-655-6100

Dallas National Decorative Accessories Show.............................800-272-SHOW

Denver Western & English Market - Denver Merchandise Mart.......303-295-1040

Denver Merchandise & Gift Show - Denver Merchandise Mart.........800-289-6278

Fashion Accessories Expo - Javits Center - New York......................203-853-6015

Fashion Jewelry World Expo - Providence, R. I...........................800-444-6572

Florida Gift Show - Orlando, Florida....................................404-220-3000

Gatlinburg Gift & Variety Show - Gatlinburg, Tn.........................423-436-6151

Gem & Lapidary Wholesalers Show...601-879-8832

Gem, Mineral Fossil Jewelry Show...602-998-4000.

Gift Source West - Las Vegas...800-325-6587

Global Leather Show...202-789-1420

Heart of America Gift Show - Branson, Mo................................417-724-8886

Imprinted Sportswear Show - nationwide..................................888-218-3912

Imprinting Business & Embroidery Show...................................908-769-1160

Indianapolis Gift Show, Lebanon, Ind....................................317-452-4202

International Boutique Show - Javits Center - New York..................617-964-5100

International Gem & Jewelry Show - Nationwide...........................301-294-1640

International Fashion Jewelry Show - Providence, R. I....................212-631-0333

International Juvenile Products Show.....................................609-231-8500

JA International Jewelry Show - Javits Center - New York...............800-829-3976

Just Kid Stuff - West...914-421-3200

Kansas City Gift Mart...800-950-MART

Las Vegas Merchandise Expo...800-421-4511

Leisure Expo - Orlando, Fl...305-448-7976

Los Angeles Gift Show - Merchandise Mart...............................800-LAMART-4

Louisville Gift Show - Louisville, Ky...502-267-7663

MAGIC - East - Javits Center- New York.....................................978-474-1900

MAGIC - Las Vegas..978-474-1900

Memphis Gift & Jewelry Show - Memphis, Tn.............................630-241-9856

Miami Gift Show - Miami Merchandise Mart - Miami, Fl.................305-261-2900

Michigan Gift Show - Northville, Mi...800-886-6247

Mid-South Jewelry & Accessories Fair - Memphis, Tn.....................630-241-9865

Minneapolis Gift Show - Minneapolis Gift Mart...............................800-626-1298

Mode Accessories Show - Toronto, Canada....................................416-510-0114

National Merchandise Show - Javits Center - New York...................800-950-1314

National Stationery Show - Javits Center- New York....................800-272-SHOW

New Orleans Gift & Jewelry Show - Superdome 630-241-9865

New York International Gift Fair - Javits Center - New York...........914-421-3224

Oasis Gift Show - Phoenix, Az...602-952-2050

Ocean City Gift Show - Ocean City, Md...410-521-7211

Off-Price Specialist Show - nationwide..414-781-6300

Ohio Gift Show - Columbus. Ohio...740-452-4541

Philadelphia Gift Show - Ft. Washington, Pa..................................770-952-6444

Pittsburgh Gift Show - Pittsburgh, Pa...716-254-2580

Portland Gift Show - Portland, Or..415-346-6666

Premium Show - Javits Center - New York......................................703-318-0300

Private Label Expo - Javits Center - New York...............................212-986-1811

Professional Golf Association Merchandise Show............................407-624-8400

Salt Lake Gift Show - Convention Center - Salt Lake, Utah..............801-973-7800

San Antonio Gift Show - San Antonio, Texas.................................512-261-4223

San Francisco International Gift Fair...914-421-3200

Santa Fe Gift Show - Santa Fe, N.M..505-989-8127

St. Louis Gift Show, Collinsville, Il...513-861-2560

Seattle Gift Show - Seattle Center..415-346-6666

Ski Industries America Outdoor Sports Show - Las Vegas................703-556-9020

Southern Ideal Home Show - Charlotte, N.C....................................800-849-0248

Southern Women's Show - nationwide..800-849-0248

Souvenir Super Show - Las Vegas..800-325-6587

Store Fixturing Show - Chicago, Il..404-252-8831

Style Industrie - Javits Center - New York..212-741-3653

Surf Expo - Florida...404-220-3000

Toy Fair - Javits Center - New York..212-675-1142

United Jewelry Show - Providence, R. I..401-331-7630

Variety Merchandise Show - Javits Center - New York....................800-950-1314

Visual Marketing & Store Design Show - New York........................212-620-0034

Washington Gift Show - Chantilly, Va...914-421-3200

Western English World Trade Show - Washington, Pa.....................203-358-9900

Accountants Are Assets

A recent study of some thirty-eight accountants nationwide, showed most would prefer to work with an account year-round, but the majority of clients are only interested at tax time. *"The most crucial problem accountants face in their relationships with small businesses is that the client does not ask for help soon enough,"* one expert stated.

CPA's contend that brink-of-disaster situations can usually be avoided if clients will force themselves to be realistic and plan ahead.

"Small businesses often spread themselves too thin and if they are trying to do everything themselves, it will never work. The key is prioritizing what will yield the most benefit." That almost sounds like my T.J. theory of operating a business: *"Do what you do best and hire somebody to do the rest!"*

Accountants listed 10 signs of trouble:

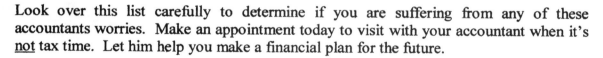

- *Poor financial planning*
- *No strategic plan*
- *Dependence on borrowed funds*
- *Overburdened management*
- *Poor financial forecasts*
- *Lag between sales growth and profit growth*
- *Poor to no cash management*
- *Late with payroll/tax deposits*
- *Inability to change, adapt, or upgrade*
- *Inability to recognize company shortcomings*

Look over this list carefully to determine if you are suffering from any of these accountants worries. Make an appointment today to visit with your accountant when it's not tax time. Let him help you make a financial plan for the future.

S.C.O.R.E. Can Create A Winner

Many times when financial problems occur, a small storeowner does not have the resources to hire the help they need. In 1973, my store was barely three years old and I felt like I was drowning. I was in debt; I was understaffed and overworked; I felt on the brink of bankruptcy with nowhere to turn. Luckily, a friend gave me the phone number of the local SBA S.C.O.R.E. office, and the rest is history.

If you need assistance, seek advice today from a real pro who has volunteered his or her services to help small retailers just like you. S.C.O.R.E., which stands for Service Corps of Retired Executives, is a *free* service which will match you with a retired business executive with experience in your field. They will meet with you as often as necessary, and as many times as needed.

Dial 1–800–634–0245, and hopefully you'll have the same success I did when I made the call.

What Are The Basic $$$ Figures of Success?

In my first book, **What Mother Never Told Ya About Retail**, I constantly confessed I am not a financial facts and figures person. That is why I relied on my wonderful CPA Lee Gray, the nice folks at S.C.O.R.E. and my retail consultant and savior, Larry Hill of RMSA. Still, I knew the conventional wisdom of a typical independent retailers income statement enough to keep my expectations at a 10% level.

TOTAL SALES	100%
Cost of Sales	52%
Gross Margin	48%
Rent Expense	10%
Payroll expense	14%
Other Expenses	14%
NET PROFIT	10%

Can you do better than that? Yes, but it's not easy, considering the low figure I have included for rent and the even lower calculation for payroll expenses. It is almost imperative that you do not allow your payroll and rent combined to exceed 25% - *unless,* and this is the *big unless,* you can raise your markup, thereby lowering your cost of sales. (This is one of the true secrets to success in retailing: *Buy low - sell high*!)

Small retailers can not afford to cut payroll costs. Good customer service is your way of competing with the biggies - the mass merchants who cut price and carry huge assortments. You must pay enough to have experienced, educated, knowledgeable and caring sales people on the floor at all times.

Advertising expenses are going to run anywhere from 3 to 7% - higher for a new store trying to get established and become known in the community. These figures probably can't be sliced either, but select your mediums carefully. I firmly believe in direct mail as the way to go, but first, you will have to succeed in compiling a mailing list.

I repeat, these are my only financial facts and figures included for you. Seek professional help; it's your money - protect it.

What Should an Employee Cost?
An Easy Way to Calculate Selling Expenses

The cost of doing business rises annually with little left over for net profit. Unfortunately when the year-end figures don't look too hot the first inclination is to cut staff. Before undertaking such a move, determine the cost and value of each person on your sales floor by using the information below, furnished to me by Rilla Clore of RMSA.

If you are a small store with less than ten employees (which I imagine *almost all* of my readers are), you must remember to consider what additional jobs your staff is responsible for doing. These figures below are for sales associates. You mustn't overlook the additional tasks your folks may be doing such as cleaning, bookkeeping, steaming, pricing merchandise, and going to the bank!

The selling costs chart will help answer questions such as: What is the sales productivity of selling personnel? Do you know your star and weak performers? What are they costing you in time and dollars? The following chart is based on a 40-hour, 50-week work year. The sales cost figure for an employee appears at the intersection of hourly pay rate and monthly sales production.

	Annual Sales		50,000	60,000	70,000	80,000	90,000	100,000	110,000	120,000	130,000	140,000	150,000	175,000	200,000	250,000	300,000
	Monthly Sales		4,167	5,000	5,833	6.667	7,5000	8,333	9,167	10,000	10,833	11,667	12,500	14,583	16,667	20,833	25,000
	Daily Sales		200	240	280	320	360	400	440	480	520	560	600	700	800	1,000	1,200
Hourly Wage	Monthly Wage	Annual Wage	% to sales	% to sales	% to sales	% to sales	% to sales	% to sales	% to sales	% to sales	% to sales	% to sales	% to sales	% to sales	% to sales	% to sales	% to sales
5.75	958.33	11,500.00	23.00	19.17	16.43	14.38	12.78	11.50	10.45	9.58	8.85	8.21	7.67	6.57	5.75	4.60	3.83
6.00	1,000.00	12,000.00	24.00	20.00	17.14	15.00	13.33	12.00	10.91	10.00	9.23	8.57	8.00	6.86	6.00	4.80	4.00
6.25	1,041.67	12,500.00	25.00	20.83	17.86	15.63	13.89	12.50	11.35	10.42	9.62	8.93	8.33	7.14	6.25	5.00	4.16
6.50	1,083.33	13,000.00	26.00	21.67	18.57	16.25	14.44	13.00	11.82	10.83	10.00	9.29	8.67	7.43	6.50	5.20	4.33
6.75	1,125.00	13,500.00	27.00	22.50	19.29	16.88	15.00	13.50	12.27	11.25	10.38	9.64	9.00	7.71	6.75	5.40	4.50
7.00	1,667.67	14,000.00	28.00	23.33	20.00	17.50	15.56	14.00	12.73	11.67	10.77	10.00	9.33	8.00	7.00	5.60	4.66
7.25	1,208.33	14,500.00	29.00	24.17	20.71	18.13	16.11	14.50	13.18	12.08	11.15	10.36	9.67	8.29	7.25	5.80	4.83
7.50	1,250.00	15,000.00	30.00	25.00	21.43	18.75	16.67	15.00	13.64	12.50	11.54	10.71	10.00	8.57	7.50	6.00	5.00
7.75	1,291.67	15,500.00	31.00	25.83	22.14	19.38	17.22	15.50	14.09	12.92	11.92	11.07	10.33	8.86	7.75	6.20	5.16
8.00	1,333.33	16,000.00	32.00	26.67	22.86	20.00	17.78	16.00	14.55	13.33	12.31	11.43	10.67	9.14	8.00	6.40	5.33
9.00	1,500.00	18,000.00	36.00	30.00	25.71	22.50	20.00	18.00	16.36	15.00	13.85	12.86	12.00	10.29	9.00	7.20	6.00
9.50	1,583.33	19,000.00	38.00	31.67	27.14	23.75	21.11	19.00	17.27	15.83	14.62	13.57	12.67	10.86	9.50	7.60	6.33
10.00	1,666.67	20,000.00	40.00	33.33	28.57	25.00	22.22	20.00	18.18	16.67	15.38	14.29	13.33	11.43	10.00	8.00	6.66
10.50	1,750.00	21,000.00	42.00	35.00	30.00	26.25	23.33	21.00	19.09	17.50	16.15	15.00	14.00	12.00	10.50	8.40	7.00
11.00	1,833.33	22,000.00	44.00	36.66	31.42	27.50	24.44	22.00	20.00	18.33	16.92	15.71	14.66	12.57	11.00	8.80	7.33
12.00	2,000.00	24,000.00	48.00	40.00	34.28	30.00	26.66	24.00	21.81	20.00	18.46	17.14	16.00	13.71	12.00	9.60	8.00

✓ If a sales person has a cost of less than 7.5% - they deserve a raise.

✓ If a person has costs of 7.5 to 10%, they are producing normally, earning what they are paid.

✓ If you have sales people costing you 10.1 to 14.6%, their efforts should be reviewed and they need improvement. (Or are they doing additional jobs, other than just selling?)

✓ Any sales person costing more than 15% of sales is being overpaid; consider appropriate action.

The New Call of the Retailer.....CHARGE!!!!!

Retailers are beginning to use plastic more and more as a means to pay their bills, and buy some of their retail inventory.

Years ago that was considered a definite no-no. If you didn't have the money, you went to a bank, and under no conditions did a reputable retailer ever use credit cards to involve stock purchases. But times have changed, and it's important that you get your own store charge card to use in these special incidents or even on a regular basis. There are benefits to be gotten from pulling out the plastic! There are numerous good, small manufacturers out there who are unable to extend you credit, but would love to ship to you. It's their credit limitations, not yours, but they accept credit cards. There are companies that can't get you approved soon enough before you will lose the order you placed; they accept credit cards. There are people who will ship an order below their minimum accepted order if you pay in advance, use a credit card. There are immediate at-once vendors across the country which you could use in person or by phone - they all accept credit cards.

All of these are so much wiser than leaving a paid-in-advance check and certainly far less expensive than C.O.D. Plus you do have a legal right to debate payment over a problem. I feel a lot safer knowing American Express or Visa is there to help in a bad situation, rather than someone having my company check ready to cash.

Here are three good reasons to pay for your inventory purchases with credit cards:

(1) _Lower freight fees and no C.O.D._ You will save a lot by not having to pay the UPS COD (which I think is now around $6.75 or so - it goes up daily!) And some companies even offer FREE freight on paid in advance orders. A credit card payment is considered a paid-in-advance, yet you won't pay it until it appears on your bill, and actually most manufacturers don't post it to the credit card account until it's shipped, so you're saving all way round.

(2) _Extra time to pay your bills_. For most retailers cash is always tight. It's no wonder, we have to pay for everything when it arrives but well before it is sold and we get our money back! Paying by credit card will handle this problem and give you a little room to breathe. In some cases, using a credit card is even better than getting an open line of credit with a firm, because your credit line will not be hurt if you pay your bill late. DO pay these accounts as soon as you can, and attempt to do it within the 25 days to avoid interest charges. When this is impossible to achieve, be certain you are using a card with the lowest possible rates and the highest possible benefits. Currently many credit cards are offering as low as 4.9 to 7.2% for the next 6 months, which is far better than you can do at the local bank or even with the SBA!

(3) Use these cards for _cash back or free trips_! Depending on the type of card you use, every purchase you make can count for free mileage trips, free gifts, special points or cash back. For example, almost every airline offers a MasterCard, Visa or American Express card that you can get so each dollar gives you a mile. Once you accumulate a certain number of miles, you exchange it for a free trip. (It can be market or _personal_!) If you use Discover Card, unfortunately I have found it is the least accepted card, so be aware many companies may not take it, you can receive up to 1 1/2% cash back on your purchases at the end of each year.

Credit Card Resource List

For airline miles
* DELTA SKYMILES which is an American Express Optima
  - that phone is 1-800-SKY-MILES.
*US Airways Dividend Miles is 1-800-9974-1660
*United Airlines Mileage Plus is 1-800-592-6700
*American Citibank Advantage is 1-800-359-4444

Read carefully each document and application.
All of these cards have a membership annual fee ranging from $35 to $50 but it's well worth it for the benefits. I found some cards which would divert your miles to several different accounts, but the only one which I felt was a good value was American Express Rewards program which is part of a regular American Express card - you just ask for the extra benefit and pay an additional small service fee.

For cash back cards here are the two I could get information on.
* There is a GE Rewards MasterCard (1-800-437-3927) which has a variable rate that's the prime plus, but gives you up to 2% cash back on all purchases.
* The Discover Card is about the same, their contact number is (1-800-347-2683).

For credit on a new car purchase there are two I am aware of:
* General Motors MasterCard (1-800-846-2273)
* Citibank Drivers Edge(1-800-967-8500)

I repeat, these are ways to help your business grow, earn extra benefits and save money - not a way to refinance or dig yourself deeper into a financial hole.

20 Suggestions for a Better Small Business

This advice is written in almost every chapter of the book, but somehow it seems more effective if it listed and marked for you to see and comprehend its importance.

✖ Have a better business plan
✖ Develop and follow a budget
✖ Know and appreciate your customer
✖ Support your community
✖ Know your own capabilities
✖ Employ people to fill the gaps
✖ Treat employees with rewards
✖ Educate employees and customers
✖ Use a data-base for marketing information
✖ Try niche marketing - 80/20 rule works
✖ Become active in the C's (Church, chamber, charity)
✖ Partner with non-competing businesses
✖ Give demonstrations of your products or service
✖ Give away free gifts and samples as advertising
✖ Use coupons and V.I.P. Buyers Clubs
✖ Build lists and awareness through contests
✖ Make your windows and displays an extra employee
✖ Be creative with your telephone messages
✖ Create an image that will last
✖ Use that image in everything

✖ Memorize the meaning of the Louisiana Cajun term: *Lagniappe* and apply it to your business daily.

La-gniappe or La-gnappe (lan-yak`) n.
1. Small gift given by a merchant to a customer for making a purchase; a bonus; something extra. 2. A gratuity; tip, something additional, that which is added. Giving more than expected.

25 Do's and Don'ts
for Succeeding in Your Small Business:

✔ Don't be too dependent on your "good" customers. They may move, die or go elsewhere.

✔ Don't expect family and friends to be your best customers. They usually aren't.

✔ Don't allow success to lower your standards - never let up, even a little.

✔ Don't assume everyone is as honest as you are; don't think everyone is dishonest either.

✔ Don't try to sell someone with good taste something is not.

✔ Don't forget someone will always have a lower price. You need to have something other then price to sell. Why not quality and service?

✔ Don't forget your customer has a point of view also. Her opinion is your main concern.

✔ Do promote the strengths of your business; your competitor does.

✔ Don't think there is a short cut to success. It's hard work, if you're doing it right!

✔ Don't underestimate your own ability. Study and learn about your specialty, then have confidence in your knowledge.

✔ Don't undercut on essentials to save money. Quality & class always win in the long run.

✔ Don't lower yourself to be like the competition that you hate.

✔ Don't forget - you can never sell every one or everything. Be satisfied with your share.

✔ Do research. You can never have too much information. The trick is to learn to organize your knowledge, and use it when needed.

✔ Do target your efforts. Have a game plan and follow it.

✔ Do treat lookers with respect, and with the expectation they'll become customers.

✔ Do treat everyone with the same dignity you expect for yourself. This includes customers, employees, co-workers, and even the competition.

✔ Do put the customers needs first - then determine how your capability can fill those needs.

✔ Do deliver more than you promise! Stretch your capabilities to the highest of your ability!

✔ Do greet each day with a smile. This is not just a job - it's your life - enjoy it!

IMAGE *from A to Z*

(What do you want to convey?)

Below are words which could be used to describe your business. Look at each carefully and decide what best represents your message to your customers and the public, in general.

Accessorized	Fun	Quiet
Amazing	Gorgeous	Regal
Aromatic	Graceful	Reliable
Artistic	Gracious	Rich
Avant-Garde	High-Fashion	Romantic
Beautiful	Hip	Sassy
Bold	Informal	Serious
Business-like	In-the-know	Slick
Casual	Jazzy	Strong
Classy	Kicky	Successful
Contemporary	Kindly	Traditional
Convenient	Literary	Trustworthy
Creative	Mild Mannered	Under-stated
Cutesy	Missy	Up-scale
Cutting Edge	No-nonsense	Visionary
Dainty	Official	Vibrant
Dashing	Old-Fashioned	Warm
Dignified	Patriotic	Well-established
Dynamic	Petite	Wacky
Efficient	Playful	Whimsical
Elegant	Practical	Wild
Elite	Professional	Wonderful
Exclusive	Preppie	X-rated
Folksy	Progressive	Youthful
Formal	Prosperous	Zany
Friendly	Quaint	

The IMAGE *of Your Business*

I have been presenting many seminars lately, especially in the gift industry, on the topic of "Creating Your Business Image." Last month there were over 300 in attendance at an evening event in Denver. The topic has been very well received, and it seems there are many store owners out there who are so busy worrying about buying and selling, they are taking little time to consider how their business is perceived. Thought must be given to everything from giftwrap selection to the color of your direct mail cards. All of these things combined make up the total IMAGE - who you are in business.

I have always broken down the word image into the following classifications:

I = Ideas and Imagination
M = Marketing and Management
A = Attitude and Advertising
G = Goal and Growth
E = Employees and Enthusiasm

Today I was delighted to receive a fax from Debbie Allen, the Best of the West correspondent for FASHION ADVANTAGE, telling about a new holiday listed in Chase's Annual Events. The entire month of May has been designated "National Business Image Awareness Month," thanks to Debbie and her efforts. See what she has to say about this event:

"The image of your business sets the tone to how successful your company can be. Just as others judge within the first few seconds of meeting, we do the same for a business. Good visual marketing takes a constant awareness! The key is to have a clear focus when walking into your business. The best business owners protect their image everywhere within their company, starting with their business cards. They continue to show a positive image throughout their advertising and promotions, signage and staff.

What does your business image project?

I   *Innovation approach to your marketing?*
M   *Motivated to make necessary changes.*
A   *Appearance sets a positive attitude.*
G   *Great displays that sell merchandise.*
E   *Entertainment marketing & selling.*

Step outside of your business and look at EVERY detail as if you were looking at it for the very first time!" says Debbie.

*(To receive more information on how to improve your business image or to receive a FREE business card evaluation, contact: Debbie Allen's Image Dynamics at (800) 359-4544 or fax (602)948-7487 or E-mail dallen7001@aol.com. Her new website is **www:businessmotivator.com**.)*

What Kind of Store Do You Have?

Perspective store owners never seem to know how to describe their business plan. When asked *"What type of store are you planning to open?"*, they will answer. *"A clothing store."* Since there are so many different categories and varieties of fashion, you first need to decide what you plan to sell before making your grand opening plans.

These information definitions were given to me by RMSA. Look over the list and see if you can determine what type of store you have or are planning to open. I realize everyone thinks theirs is very special, unique and entirely different from any other in the world, but basically all stores have to fit into one of these categories. The biggest mistake you can make is trying to be everything to everybody. Please define your niche and build your business around that area.

TRADITIONAL: This type of store carries clothing that changes very little, season after season. Investment clothing is the staple of this type of store. Merchandise tends to be very classic and is not affected by passing fads or trends.

UPDATED TRADITIONAL: This type of store carries clothing that is still very classic in design, but with more fashion forward basics to update the traditional basics, i.e. women's mini/long skirts, etc. Merchandise is influenced by what is happening in the fashion world.

CONVENTIONAL: This store caters to middle America, with a predominance of branded merchandise usually at moderate price points. It could carry some fashion merchandise, along with the very basic types of merchandise.

CONTEMPORARY: This store receives all of the latest fashion trends. The styles are usually a season earlier than in other types of stores. Very updated merchandise mix. The fashion looks are usually influenced by the latest trends. Faster turning merchandise than most of the other store types. Price points may vary from moderate to upper better.

EUROPEAN: This type of store is very trendy, sophisticated and influenced by the European market and designers. Usually very high fashion and fast turning, typically at better price points.

DESIGNER: This store carries designer labels only, usually a designer's couture line.

ACTIVE SPORTSWEAR: This store has clothing that you wear while performing a sport or want to look like you are a participant in a sport (golf, tennis, running, workout, etc.).. This store may also include equipment to be used while performing a particular sport.

WESTERN: This type of store carries western (and English) clothing along with boots, hats, and occasionally, saddles and tack.

ACCESSORY: A store that carries only accessory items such as belts, bags, jewelry, hats. If there is apparel, it is generally one-size-fits-all, wraps, and very casual wear items.

Attitude and In the Pursuit of Excellence,

A poor image can and must be improved in today's marketplace. Top professionals tell us that attitude and image takes something more than just saying to ourselves, "I'll do the best I can." We must be better than our best. In any field or sport, a professional is one who loves the game, is proficient at it and plays it for keeps. Perhaps more important than anything else, they never quit, no matter what the odds. You find professionals give a little extra effort in order to excel, to come out on top. This surge usually makes the difference in any kind of competition. It starts with attitude.

To Be Your Best Requires "ATTITUDE"

A mbition (a goal in life)
T act (good manners/customer service)
T raining (product knowledge)
I nterest (caring about the customer)
T houghtfulness (showing you care)
U nderstanding (empathy)
D esire (a true interest/concern)
E nthusiasm (excitement, energy)
S incerity (honestly meaning it!)

What is YOURS?

Today's top employees in all fields of service must possess certain qualities that make the dollar difference and portray a professional image. Those basic qualities are:

(1) Personality
(2) Effort
(3) Knowledge

Just building on these three traits, a person can become a successful sales representative for your business and also a happy, likeable member of society. It is as always, mind over matter. People become what they think about all day long. Those who worry become tense, harsh, abrasive while those who have a happy outlook generally are cheerful, helpful and good-natured.

The old song, *"Accentuate the Positive"* is still true. Avoid negative words in your mind like I hope, I might and I wish. Replace them with positive thoughts like I can, I will, I will.

Say What You Mean, Mean What You Say - Carefully!

Do you think before you speak, does your mouth go into action before your mind goes into gear? Don't feel bad, we all have this problem, but to maintain a successful and profitable business relationship we need to watch our language - not just as in four-letter words, but by carefully selecting the phrases we use in dealing with a customer. Your choice of words could be the difference in an angry consumer or a satisfied customer.

Angry customers not only don't return to spend money, they tell all their friends, relatives, and anyone else who'll listen to them. It's best to prevent the problem in the beginning with smooth language and good customer service matters.

Avoid the following phrases:

*"**You have to...**"* - Do they really? Of course not. My natural reaction to that sentence would be, *"You wanna bet?"* The customer doesn't *have to* do anything you say; they have the option of going somewhere else. (Lots of *somewheres!*) Instead say, *"Would you please..."* Or *"May I ask you to..."* Isn't that a much nicer way to say the same thing?

*"**I'll try...**"* - Are you serious? Sounds like a brush off to me. Customers demand and deserve a direct answer such as: *"I'll find out and get right back with you,"* or *"I feel sure I can do this, but I must check with the manager."* Don't ever just offer *"to try."* Do something, say something to let them know you really mean to help them any way you possibly can - then actually do it.

*"**But...**"* This is such a dead-end word - a negative word with no real meaning. Use *"however"* instead. It offers a smoother alternative and leaves open options that sound positive, and less argumentative.

*"**It is against our policy...**"* Customers who are really angry are in no mood to hear about your company policy. If you must deal in this matter, point out the rules by leaving out the word *"policy."* Instead say *"procedure"* or *"approach"* or even *"This is the way we usually handle these matters."*

Don't give the appearance of a cold unconcerned major corporation in dealing with the public. With each customer make every effort to appear warm, personal, and at all times in agreement with them! People like folks who agree with them. They tend to return and spend money with people who understand they way they feel about things.

Think Before Signing a Lease
Seek Legal Advice

When you first consider opening a store, you visualize the most beautiful location in the world. Then after the first planning stage, a future retailer usually finds out they need money for inventory more than for fancy fixtures, couches and espresso machines. After looking around at vacant buildings and meeting with Realtors for weeks, sometimes months, you eventually may have to settle for less than you had planned. Or perhaps your successful business has grown so much you are bursting at the seams, and now are in need of a larger facility. (Congratulations!)

Whatever your physical location need, here are a few things to watch for before signing your name to the dotted line of a lease:

✓ Does the lease contain a renewal clause? You want to leave when *you are* ready, not when the landlord decides to do something else with the property

✓ Who will bear the rsponsibility for building repairs and maintenance? Spell it out, or you may be unpleasantly surprised when the water heater bursts next winter, or the wall-to-wall carpet needs cleaning, or worse yet - replacing.

✓ Are there restrictions on the signs you can put up? Make sure your style and size requirements can be accomodated. Can you display on the sidewalk for special events? Is there a sign for use by merchants within the center?

✓ If you are in a center, is there a merchants group that you are required to join? Is there a monthly advertising fee, or a merchants promotion fund which you must contribute to? Are there special hours that you must adhere to, or can you set your own closing time?

✓ Is there enough parking to meet your company's needs now and in the future? Do you share the lot with another business? Who is responsible for maintenance of the parking area?

✓ If there is grass and shrubbery, whose responsibility is the upkeep and service to care for these? Who pays for the garbage pickup ?

✓ Who pays for termite and pest control?

No matter how silly or insignificant something seems, add it to the lease. This is a legal document; it is better to be safe than sorry. You may want to pay a little more for a shorter term lease if there are any unanaswered questions in your mind about the proposition. Don't lock yourself into any situation that doesn't fit your needs or meet your expectations.

To Mall or Not To Mall ? That is the Question

When business is bad or even not as good as a store owner anticipated, they seem to get in a *moving* mode. A simple drop in sales one month and the thought of changing locations becomes a burning question. Retailers start looking at vacant buildings, checking out the new strip centers across town, and pricing build-outs in new malls...then they seem to want another person's viewpoint and they call me.

It's very difficult to know where just the right place for the *perfect* women's specialty store is. If I had that answer, I'd be there making extra trips each day to the bank. There are a few considerations I can suggest to anyone weighing their options in the real estate game.

The Pros of Being In A Mall:

There should be ready-made traffic at all hours of the day and evening. Retailers enjoy the benefit of mall advertising and promotions. There are greater opportunities for expansion into other similar malls. There are constant opportunities for cross-promotions and special events with other mall stores. The specialty shop should be easily discovered by customers already shopping elsewhere in the mall. Customers feel safer in a mall environment. Parking is readily available.

The Cons of Being In A Mall:

The rent is usually much much more than a small retailer pays elsewhere. There are many extra location and maintenance fees involved in the lease, as well as overage, ad co-ops, etc. Some shoppers do not enjoy shopping in big centers and avoid them at all costs. It is possible a store will lose some of their regular trade to this problem. All stores have to keep the same mall hours which usually involves 7 days a week, including evenings. Most small independent store owners do not have the employee base for this type of schedule and can not possibly maintain this work lifestyle themselves. You will be forced to hire additional employees and relinquish some of the management control to other people.

When making a decision as important as a location change, weigh all the options carefully. Discuss the matter with your employees, your customers, your banker, and your family. Will the additional costs and time sacrifices be worth the additional income? Will the additional sales be eaten up by bigger salaries, higher rents, and more expenses?

Remember specialty store means being SPECIAL to your customers, and feeling special about yourself! Wherever you go, make sure you maintain that image.

The Construction Zone -
How To Survive Renovation Projects

Life is good. The store looks great; inventory is just right, and customers are spending money. As Mr Rogers would say, *"It's a wonderful day in the neighborhood."* Then it starts - downtown renovation.

More business has been lost in the name of progress than any other plague known to man. Retailers can have been running successful businesses for years, but when the bulldozers and the jackhammers arrive outside the door, their sales plummet, customers abandon ship and retailers panic.

But it doesn't have to be that way. With careful planning I have known stores who have turned their construction projects into profitable promotions. It just takes a little creativity to twist this retail lemon into a thirst quenching sales campaign.

Project the worst possible scenario. Mark your calendar for the days when the streets will be totally blocked or the front sidewalk completely destroyed. It may prove less stressful, less expensive and more sensible to close the doors for that short period. Plan vacation periods or give your staff the time off with pay and tell them you expect them to give double-duty efforts later when you have the re-opening rush.

Treat customers extra-special during these trying times. Realize they are probably driving through gravel, dodging ladders, and perhaps passing wolf-whistling construction guys to get to you. Send those who do brave the elements a personalized thank you note for entering the demolition zone. Add a future discount coupon or appreciation offer for their return visit when things are back to normal..

Plan new routes to your door. If the access roads have detours or there is a better way to find you, let the customers know. Draw a map, use signage to point the way. Play a little game of "Who can find the door?" Tape cut-out construction paper footprints on the sidewalk leading to your temporary entrance. Use ladders, paint cans, hammers, construction zone tape and road signs in your windows displays if they are still visible to passersby. If not, put up billboards or posters that say, *"We're still in here - come see! Just follow the signs."*

Join other merchants in helping each other. Publish a newsletter to keep customers aware of what's happening. Plan events that will direct shoppers from one store to another. This is a great time for a Scavenger Hunt that requires buyers to have their card validated at each location before dropping it in to enter a giveaway contest. Have a back door party in the alley and serve refreshments. Hire someone to be the guide, leading customers to your temporary entrances. They could be sort of like a Walmart greeter (but better dressed) - welcoming customers, telling them about today's values and then assisting in carrying their purchases back to the car.

Keep everyone that could be affected posted on your problems. Vendors will understand if warned in advance. They want to protect your business for the future so if you have to cut back on orders or delay shipments they should understand. If they don't, I think I would reconsider that supplier relationship.

Delivery people need to know where and when they can bring in your shipments. Your local bank should be well aware of the problems, but talk to them anyway. Ask for a little extra time on that note payment. They live there, too. Most will gladly co-operate - but *only* if you ask.

Enlist all merchants to participate in the "Excuse Our Mess" campaign. Make joint purchases of shopping bags featuring construction logos and purchase ad spots as a group. Don't forget to take pictures of the before, the after and of course, the *during,* to use on bulletin boards and in advertising.

Promotions can involve everything from discounts for wearing a construction hard hat to guessing the number of days the door will be blocked. John Buster of the D & J Store in Guymon, Oklahoma took full advantage of a similar problem in his community a few years back. When the sidewalk outside his family-owned department store was broken up for replacement, he recovered big chunks of the concrete, spray painted them gold and sold *"Pieces of Guymon's History"* for only $25.00 with an official certificate of authenticity attached. Yes, it was a joke, and amused local folks paid $25 for a hunk of sidewalk, knowing their donation was going to the Downtown Merchants Association fund for goodwill. John had a great time on the radio telling folks to rush in to get the last remnants of the town's past memories, and shoppers came down to see for themselves, plus buy a few things since they were there anyway. This is what happens you when think positively and make the best of what life sends you.

Turn your troubles into fun, and under no circumstances do you ever complain to customers about your inconvenience. The construction is probably being done in the name of civic beautification or community renovation, so put a smile on your face and be proud, because progress usually means profits.

Slap that hardhat on your head and begin to construct your own blueprint to meet the challenge.

Please Touch the Merchandise!

The other day I was in a store that was so full of signs, I couldn't concentrate on shopping for reading. There was " no this", "no that", and "don't do this", and "we don't allow that." I thought I would go nuts trying to figure out exactly what I could "DO" in this place. There were just "don'ts!"

But...the store was spotless - so clean it almost sparkled. Actually, a better descriptive word would be *sterile*. Know what that means? Antiseptic, which also equals empty. These people were so concerned with not allowing the customers to touch, hold, move, etc., that no one felt comfortable enough to stay in the store very long.

I was immediately reminded of a store in Lake Tahoe in the Harvey Resort Shopping Mall that posts a sign that reads just the reverse: *If you are barefooted, shirtless, smoking, eating a hamburger, drinking a coke, and carrying a crying baby - you're welcome here!* Yes, they wanted everybody's business! Anyone could feel at ease in that place, and did.

Now I agree that carries things a little too far, but remember - we are not in business to have a perfect, clean spotless atmosphere to show off. We're there to sell things to people, hopefully at a profit. And people like to touch. Watch customers walk around in the store. They'll look at items, then get closer, and reach out to touch, to feel, to rub. This is the final closeness that makes the sale. That's what puts the customer *"in touch"* so to speak. That's why it's so important to get them into the dressing rooms to try on items.

If an item is handled, it is twice as likely to be purchased. When a customer can identify with a product, it becomes theirs - or at least it becomes the object of their desire. Here are three examples to encourage your customers to touch and feel and try on:

(1) Eliminate showcases whenever possible. Put all inventory in open racks and cases where it is easy to get to.

(2) Remove any extra packaging or plastic bags which will interfere with customer touch. Who are you saving it for? I never buy anything in a store which has it's merchandise covered with plastic bags; I assume it's been here forever!

(3) Be knowledgeable about your own inventory so you can answer any customer's questions about the feel and touch. Know the fabric content, the care and wearability.

Encourage your staff members to play the *"touch"* game. Blindfold the employee and ask them to feel the fabric. See if they can correctly identify the fabric and/or the garment. Just involving them in this role-play game will increase their attention to details and to having the customers *feel* the merchandise.

Try it yourself - you'll like it!

Technology and Change - Still the Key to Profits!

As we enter the 21st century, many retailers continue from day to day to do the same thing, in the same manner, in the same place and expect the same results. Unfortunately, it doesn't work that way anymore. Just like twice-a-year clearance sales, 9 to 5 store hours, and keystone mark-ups, most of your current retail attitudes and actions will become obsolete by the year 2010.

Times change, people change and most importantly their shopping attitudes change with their lifestyles. The problem with the majority of small retailers is their inability to cope with change in any form, which is leaving today's store owners watching their sales dwindle and their profits decline while they are trying to figure out what they're doing wrong. Yet *doing wrong* is not the problem. *Keeping up* the pace and *staying in tune* and *in touch* is the culprit.

Less than 1/3 of today's small retailers have opted to purchase a computer system. Many consider the investment too steep, but the main reason is the fear of technology and learning to use the machine. Although almost every grade school child is knowledgeable in computer by age seven, most forty year olds are afraid to venture into the world of computer jargon. Store owners would rather spend extra hours in the office at their desk (away from the selling floor) to handle orders, bookkeeping, payroll, etc. which could be done in a matter of minutes on a computer. Software, computers, and printers are available now in a complete retail set-up at less than $5,000. This is basically the salary a retailer is having to pay that extra sales assistant to take their place in the store. (And that part-time employee is not offering the same excellent friendly service or personalized attention that the presence of an owner gives.)

With the technology of a computer system and a simple database of the customers, today's retailer could have a wonderland of knowledge concerning not only their customer's buying patterns but their likes, their dislikes, their birthdays, family members, and other important elements that make a customer more apt to shop one store over the other.

With the capability of a computer mail-label system, a store owner could reach their customer base in a matter of minutes by simply making a quick label run for direct mail purposes. The label list could be divided into categories and demographics which would eliminate waste and save store owners hundreds of dollars in excess postage by being able to reach just those customers to which a particular mailing would apply.

With the mathematical genius of a computer and the correct retail software, a buyer would realize which lines are selling, at what turn-over periods, at what markups, in what quantities and therefore save thousands of dollars in markdowns and excess inventory. One season of better buying because of accurate and more precise information would actually pay for the cost of the entire system.

Now does the word computer still sound too complicated and out of reach for the small retailer? Of course not. This is the wave of the future - NO; it's the basic reality of today and only those who are actively pursuing timely information and using it to implement change within their stores are remaining successful and on top of the market.

The customer of the future will expect - will require, personalized, individual service from an informed retailer. The only way you can achieve both of these tasks is through the use of technology that is readily and economically available to you.

Pick up your mouse and go for it!

Surveys: Ask and Ye Shall Receive.....An Answer!

Research is not limited to major corporations in today's business world. Even the smallest corner store or local deli needs information on which to base business changes. You need research to determine how your competition is doing; you need research to see how your market is changing; you need research to find out what your customers want; you need research to learn how to improve your business. Where do you get these answers? You do a SURVEY!

Surveys can be conducted in numerous ways: direct in person, by mail, by fax, or by phone. Generally, you will get a better response if you ask customers to complete the surveys while on your premises. Follow the guidelines below, and above all, let your customers know how you have implemented their suggestions. Eight of ten will come back to see if you have followed their advice.

- Keep surveys simple and easy to read. Do not get too technical. Do not get too personal. Don't make the survey too long or boring.

- Ask close-ended or direct questions as much as possible. Offer them a choice of categories to check. Use multiple choice answers if applicable.

- Get a large sample before you tabulate results. Ten surveys will not give you an accurate presentation. The number needed will be determined by the size of your business.

- Put yourself in the customer's place. Can they furnish the info you're asking for?

- Leave plenty of room if you asked open ended questions, or if one of your answers is *"other."* The extra space will encourage customers to elaborate.

- Give respondents some kind of reward or incentive for completing your survey. examples include a coupon redeemable on their next purchase or a grand prize drawing to be drawn at the end of the survey period.

- Construct the survey so that the results can be utilized in as many ways as possible. For example, if names and addresses are used, they can be added to your mailing list. Ages can be used to determine target customer age category, therefore aiding in determining what type of advertising medium to choose.

You will constantly need to upgrade your mailing list, but I suggest you frequently do surveys that do not require the participant to identify themselves. Surveys that ask questions about income or general demographics do not need the respondent's name and address. Also do not expect a customer to criticize you or an employee if their name is required on the form.

Design the survey form which will best suit you and your business. There are two examples on the next pages. One is applicable to the clothing industry; the other is designed for gift and housewares retailers.

Gift Shop survey

Help us help you!

(Add your store name and logo here)

___Please help us to better serve you and your special needs by taking a minute or two to answer the following questions. This is your opportunity to tell us what you expect and want from our store. Thank you so much!

___

1. What is your age? _____18-24 _____25-39 _____40-54 _____55-64 _____65 and over

2. What is your occupation?___Professional ____Managerial_____Clerical____Homemaker
          ____Other _____Home office

3. Which size category do you purchase most? ___Gifts ___Housewares ___Gourmet ____Collectibles

4. Where do you shop most? ___Malls ___Dept. Stores ___Small Stores___Discount stores___Catalogs____TV

5. What features determine where you shop? (You may check more than one.) ___Price ___Location
      ____Service available ____Latest fashion ____Advertising ___Store decor/mood ___Store hours

6. How much do you spend on gifts//housewares each year?
      _____under $300 _____$300-500 ___$501-$1000 ____$1000-$2000 ____over $2000

7. What is your combined family income? ___under $25,000 ___$25-40,000 ___$41-60,000 ___over

8. What do you like most about our store?

9. What do you not like?

10. What brands would you like us to add that we don't carry?
_____   _____   _____
_____   _____   _____

Please add any additional comments that will help us serve you better! (You do not have to sign your name!)

Name:_____ Address:_____

Date in Store:_____ Phone_____

40

Clothing Store survey

Help us help you!

(Add your store name and logo here)

___*Please help us to better serve you and your special needs by taking a minute or two to answer the following questions. This is your opportunity to tell us what you expect and want from our store. Thank you so much!*

___

1. *What is your age?* ____ *18-24* _____ *25-39* _____ *40-54* _____ *55-64* _____ *65 and over*

2. *What is your occupation?* ___*Professional* ____*Managerial* _____*Clerical* ____*Homemaker* ____*Other* _____*Home office*

3. *Which size category do you purchase most?* ___*Juniors* ___*Misses* ___*Petites* ____*Plus sizes*

4. *Where do you shop most?* ___*Malls* ___*Dept. Stores* ___*Small Stores* ___*Discount stores* ___*Catalogs* ____*TV*

5. *What features determine where you shop? (You may check more than one.)* ___*Price* ___*Location* ____*Service available* ____*Latest fashion* ____*Advertising* ___*Store decor/mood* ___*Store hours*

6. *How much do you spend on clothing each year (excluding shoes)?* _____*under $300* _____*$300-500* ___*$501-$1000* ____*$1000-$2000* ____*over $2000*

7. *What is your combined family income?* ___*under $25,000* ___*$25-40,000* ___*$41-60,000* ___*over*

8. *What categories (in order 1-5) do you spend the most for?* ___*Suits/Career* ___*Dresses*

   ___*Casual sportswear* ____*Very casual sportswear* ____*Other - please list*_____

9. *What price do you expect to pay for the following (on average)?* _____*Casual Set* _____*Slacks* _____*Sweater*_____*Blouse*_____*Skirts*_____*Blazer*_____*Jeans*____*Knit top* _____*Dress*_____*Suit*_____*Winter Coat*_____*Evening Dress*_____*Earrings* _____*Handbag*

10. *What do you like most about our store?* _____
_____
_____
_____
____

11. *What do you not like?* _____
_____
_____
_____

12. *What brands would you like us to add that we don't carry?*
_____   _____   _____
_____   _____   _____

Please add any additional comments that will help us serve you better! (You do not have to sign your name!)

The ☆T.J. Test.....
100 Retail Questions

1. Is your store easy to locate?
2. Do you provide mailers, instructions, brochures?
3. Is your landscaping, parking lot, outside area appealing?
4. Is parking lot safe, clean, large enough?
5. Are your windows visible from the street?
6. Are they clean, neat and well decorated?
7. Do you change windows at least every 10 days?
8. Is your entrance view a complete scope of the store?
9. Does your layout invite "movement" through the store?
10. Are aisle ways free of boxes, clutter?
11. Are racks and shelves at the proper height for the average customer?
12. Do you use indoor display?
13. Is your store name visible at least six times inside the store?
14. Do your bags, tags, and sales tickets follow your image?
15. Are your store policies clearly displayed? (Framed? Professionally printed?)
16. Does your staff greet customers within 30 seconds?
17. Are there at least 2 sales associates on the floor at all times?
18. Is there someone on hand empowered to handle *any* problem that may arise?
19. Is your sales staff "trained" to sell and demonstrate your products?
20. Do you have regular store meetings to educate and motivate?
21. Do you offer credit card charges?
22. Do you offer in-store charges?
23. Do you offer giftwrap services? Free ?
24. Do you offer alterations on apparel? Free?
25. Do you offer delivery services?
26. Do you offer after-hours shopping/consultations?
27. Do you have personal shoppers?
28. Do you offer UPS/mail shipping for customers?
29. Do you do closet cleaning?
30. Do you have private label bath/body products?
31. Do you publish a store newsletter?

32. Do you use direct mail on a regular basis?

33. Do you have a 'complete' customer mailing list?

34. Do you offer a frequent buyer club?

35. Do you have a birthday club?

36. Have you tried an earring club? Hosiery club?

37. Do you present style shows/seminars?

38. Have you sponsored an advisory board or focus group?

39. Have you used a store survey?

40. Do you join in chamber/mall sponsored events?

41. Do you serve on chamber/civic committees?

42. Have you sponsored any school related programs in your community?

43. Do you offer a senior citizens discount or special discount day?

44. Do you go to market a minimum of 3 times a year?

45. Do you subscribe to fashion publications, newsletters?

46. Do you have a computer? Fashion software? OTB software? Mail list capability?

47. Do you have an Open to Buy for each season?

48. Do you know your markup percentage?

49. Do you know your maintained markup?

50. Are you aware of your break-even point?

51. Did you set sales goals for the store? For employees?

52. Do you have an advertising budget?

53. Do you have an annual advertising plan?

54. Do you have a seasonal display plan?

55. Do you have a visuals and display budget?

56. Have you ever videoed your store?

57. Do you take at least one day off?

58. Do you "visually" shop similar stores at least once a month?

59. Do you shop *at-home?*

60. Do you reward your employees for a job well done?

61. Do you have employee incentive plans and goals?

62. Do you have an attractive, clean restroom for customers/staff?

63. Do you offer coffee, soft drinks?

64. Do you have a comfortable seating area?

65. Are your dressing rooms large enough?

66. Do you have a chair in each one?

67. Do you have more than 2 hooks and a shelf in each dressing room?

68. Do you include the extras like shoulder pads, sleevebands, face shields?

69. Do you have a full-length 3 way mirror outside dressing rooms?

70. Do you have *shoes* for proper length fitting?

71. Do you carry shoes or offer referrals for items not in inventory?

72. Does each sales person have a customer book?

73. Do they make daily phone calls and follow-ups?

74. Do you send thank you notes?

75. Do you have enough insurance? Business interruption?

76. Do you fully understand your coverage?

77. Do you have fire extinguishers? Charged? Do you know where they are?

78. Do you have an answering machine? Do you set it at night for an advertisement?

79. Do you take your phone calls - even creditors?

80. Do you have a complete credit sheet to give vendors at market?

81. Do you have a business plan on file with your banker?

82. Do you have available cash-on-hand for emergencies or great deals?

83. Do you have good "retail relationships"?

84. Do you barter with fellow merchants?

85. Do you plan enough market time?

86. Do you arrive prepared with lists and appointments?

87. Do you attend seminars, workshops and style shows?

88. Do you make use of market handouts after going home?

89. Do you share your information with your staff?

90. Do you bring a camera to market?

91. Do you use these photos and information for selling?

92. Do you build seasonal boards for your store and staff?

93. Do you make customer notes on order copies?

94. Are orders completed at market?

95. Do you stay in contact with sales reps during non-market seasons?

96. Do you know the customer service reps at major companies?

97. Do you set up files on merchandise shipment schedules?

98. Do you follow-up on late deliveries?

99. Do you take markdowns early on slow sellers?

100. DO YOU LIKE WHAT YOU DO??? ☆

☆ This is probably the most important answer. Is it *"yes"*? Then, go for it!

Today's Customer Service Challenge

To deliver SUPERIOR customer service, day in and day out, you need to review the philosophy that establishes the prevailing attitude at your store concerning customer service. I believe attitude is more important than any philosophy! No matter how many employee meetings you hold or handouts you give away, if your staff is not "into" a customer service mode and their attitude is not in "gear", you are wasting your time on philosophy. They have an *Attitude!*

Your rule for delivering excellent customer service is to do it consistently each day you're open for business! NO MORE; NO LESS!! It can't just be on the days you feel good, look good, or have a great sale in progress. It can't be selectively done for "good" customers or "pretty" customers or "fun" customers, but for each and every person who walks through the door. (Remember the scene from the movie, "Pretty Woman"?)

No one ever said this would be easy. Customer satisfaction has a million definitions, each as individual and unique as the customer who defined it. What satisfies one might aggravate another. This is not a clothing or gift business - it is a people business. It always has been; it always will be. Learn to demonstrate your ability to help people and to put their happiness first. This is true customer service. It is important to remember that customer satisfaction is the single most important agenda in successful business. Customers are the only reason we are in business; that creates the bottom line.

Customers may view your store through only one transaction. When one thing is handled incorrectly, it can tarnish the entire store's reputation. Everyone takes the rap when one person is rude or doesn't know the product. To make things worse, unhappy customers tell other people. The reputation of your business can be destroyed in one conversation at the grocery store or country club. Consider for each unhappy customer, whether they complain or not, ten other people hear about the problem, either from the customer or from someone who heard it from the customer. They, in turn, pass it along whenever the opportunity presents itself and what happens each time the story is retold? Well, of course, it changes, it grows, and it multiplies! The more negative it is, the bigger and worst it becomes.

Can you name all the times that you personally pay a little more for a product or service because of the way it is delivered, or because you like the person who delivers it? The money goes where the customer believes the money is appreciated. Demonstrate a friendly atmosphere so a business relationship can exist with a friendship.

It's time to look at customer complaints as opportunities. Complaints allow us to solve the problem - fix the wrong before it is broadcast all over town. You can turn complaints into satisfaction and become a hero to some customers. Just ask! Usually if you can get the customer to tell you what is wrong, you can solve any problem.

Instill customer service in your staff by making it a priority each and every day! Mention it in memos, at parties, at meetings, post it on the wall, talk about it on the sales floor.

"IF YOU'RE NOT TAKING CARE OF YOUR CUSTOMERS, SOMEBODY ELSE WILL!"

MAKING YOURSELF A ☆
What is Your U.S.P.?
3 Little Letters That Mean $$$

What advantage is there for your customers to do business with you? What makes you unique or special? Your UNIQUE SELLING POINT (USP) is the distinguishing advantage you hold out in all of your marketing, advertising and sales efforts. It's something that a customer usually can't get anywhere else.

It's the foundation of your business, and you should make it a part of everything you do. What your USP should say depends on the specific market niche you have already carved, or wish to carve out. Your USP may be that you only sell the highest quality garments in the industry or:

✖ Your USP may be that you sell your garments at the lowest mark up in your community.

✖ Your USP may be that you are open 9 AM to 9 PM, seven days a week to service customers.

✖ Your USP may be that you have more customer service personnel than anyone else in town.

✖ Your USP may be that you provide information, education, and fashion assistance at all times.

✖ Your USP may be that you offer interest-free charge accounts and easy payment plans.

✖ Your USP may be that you offer after-hours shopping by special appointment.

✖ Your USP is NOT that you are the same as everybody else!

Too many stores try to be *"Me-Too"* businesses. They develop nothing that makes them different and nothing that creates a desire in the customer to even look for anything special in them. Too many doors just open to sell - sell - sell. You need to commit to becoming a business that's dedicated to solving people's problems. Then the sales will happen.

Perhaps that could be your USP! Decide what you are and what makes you different.   Figure out your own personal USP and start promoting its benefits to your customers and potential shoppers today!

My USP is_____

_____

_____

_____

_____

_____

_____

_____

Developing Customer Loyalty

In the Raphel's great book, **Up the Loyalty Ladder**, they talk about the five rungs of the ladder and who these people are:

(1) <u>Prospects</u> - people who may be interested in buying from you.
(2) <u>Shoppers</u> - people who visit your business at least once.
(3) <u>Customers</u> - people who purchase one or more products from you
(4) <u>Clients</u> - people who regularly purchase your products.
(5) <u>Advocates</u> - people who tell anyone who will listen how great your business is.

Wouldn't it be wonderful if your mailing list was loaded with only clients and advocates. Unfortunately, it doesn't work that way and it is your constant challenge to turn those first three types into the last two. You must learn to develop customer relationships and make retail friends.

The American Express Retail Index on shopper loyalty found that consumers consistently associate loyalty with the idea of having fun while shopping, regardless of the type of retailer they visit. 42% of customers who shop specialty stores felt it was extremely important that the store be a *"fun place to shop."* The Index also said specialty store shoppers tend to be more affluent and are seeking good values, the latest styles and fashions, and helpful courteous staff, as well as a fun place to shop.

They offered an interesting profile: Over 45% of all specialty store shoppers have four or more years of college. They spend an average of $64.00 per shopping visit, and shop your store at least once each month for about $400 every six month period. This means that a ten year loyal customer is worth over $8,000 to your business. Are you seeing dollar $igns now?

American Express broke down shoppers into three categories:

"Savvy" Shopper ❤ will pay for quality. Prefers "better" stores. This is 29% of shoppers who are 42% of sales volume.

"Recreational" Shopper ☺ shops for fun, unplanned purchases. This is 5% of shoppers - 33% of volume.

"Convenience" Shopper ☹ only shops when they need to and don't enjoy it. 36% of all shoppers who equal 25% of sales volume.

When asked, customers define loyalty much differently from the survey reports. 44% said loyalty is determined by where they do most of their shopping. 27% said it is where they think to shop first, and 7% said it is where they tend to shop *regardless of price.*

The reasons they gave for changing stores or quitting shopping at a particular business were:
- ✔ Prices tend to be too high.
- ✔ Absence of preferred styles.
- ✔ Merchandise is often out of stock.
- ✔ Racks, shelves are disorganized.
- ✔ Employees are not helpful.
- ✔ Absence of preferred brands.

What is Customer Service?

Retail advisor Sally McDevitt describes the following list as ways of providing good customer service. Why not use these ideas to improve your level of service?

- Greeting
- Approach time
- No lines
- Beyond level of service
- Knowing customer's likes & dislikes
- Special orders
- Selection of stock
- Store appearance
- Adapting to customer
- Know customer by name
- Quick check out
- Gift wrap
- Alterations
- Location of store
- Kids play area
- Wheel chair access
- Carry packages to car
- Mail orders
- Drinks or refreshments
- Umbrellas for customer use
- Return policy posted at register
- Seating area
- Good Signage
- Special in-store events
- Gifts with purchase
- Personal cards
- Thank you notes
- Buying at best price and passing on savings
- Follow through on sales
- S-M-I-L-E☺!

Service and selection bring customers back. Make it your goal to offer and have the best customer service.

Take a Stock Walk

Customer Service Advice from Sally McDevitt

A *"Stock Walk"* is a daily 15-20 minutes Morning Tour with your crew through your entire department, store and stock room. It should be directly before store opening. If your store opens at 10:00 A.M. anticipate your morning preparation time to end at 9:40 A.M. Your sales floor should be ready for the business then, and the last 20 minutes can be used for a *"Stock Walk."*

This early morning time well spent with your staff can make or break your day. It is the perfect opportunity to talk customer service, ask your crew questions and role play approaches to customers. Let each sales associate give a try selling you the garments. I.E. *"Let me show you our new JH Collectibles Group. It just arrived today."* Challenge each one; promote a little friendly competition between staff. *"I can sell 4 Carol Anderson dresses today. How many can you sell?"* *"If you beat me. You can have a weekend off."*...Get their juices flowing; selling is fun! Offer incentives and rewards for reaching goals.

Topics to discuss during your stock walk:

✔ Daily sales figures
✔ Housekeeping and appearances
✔ Displays and signage
✔ Stock awareness - Hot items and trends - this is a good time to suggest *"Hot Item of the Day"* to show every customer that walks through the door. Also discuss great price items and any commitment to value items.
✔ Advertised styles and promotions
✔ New markdowns/ competitive markdowns

The consistency of the stock walk sets a standard for good communication and clarifies your expectation level of your crew. This is a useful tool in training the staff. Merchandise awareness is a big part of a successful business. Begin to incorporate this into your management pattern and you'll soon see the successful financial results of your daily exercise.

(I met Sally McDevitt when she presented workshops for the DMCU during Women's Apparel and Gift Market. She gained much of her customer service expertise from her background with department store giant, Nordstrom's. Her wonderful enthusiasm and energy was contagious; her expertise and knowledge was priceless. Buyers were thrilled with her advice and greatly benefitted from her programs....T.J.)

Sally's Texas-based sales training and consulting firm is Retail Fashion Right. She can be reached at 972-540-5634.

What Do Women Want?
The Age Old Question Asked Once More

No matter how hard they are to understand, women are still questioned on their likes and dislikes by surveys, in focus groups, and of course, by husbands every day. The Cotton, Inc. Lifestyle Monitor took this topic seriously when they set out to interview thousands of women nationwide with a 125 question-phone survey about just what the customer wanted when shopping for clothing. The three most important categories were probed more deeply in order to better understand the current marketplace.

The answers were somewhat shocking and contradictory when they showed 55 percent of women considered selection and variety as their most important factors when choosing a store. Price came in a poor 12 percent and convenience hardly counted since only 3 percent mentioned it as factor in selection. (Where did they find these women? Or are we (the retailers) the ones who don't understand what our customers are actually looking for?)

In the *"What Do You Like To Wear Category"*, jeans won without a doubt. Women stated they were appropriate for wearing to the mall, the movies, and the supermarket. But guess what? For at-home wear when no one's around, 63% said they'd rather wear sweats!

The prices again didn't seem to be too much of a problem, although 10 percent said they would not pay more than $20 for a pair of jeans; 32 percent will pay $21 to $30, while the largest group (34 percent) will spend between $32 and $40. Going on up, 5 percent will shell out $41 to $50, and 4 percent are willing to pay even more for the perfect jean.

And what is the perfect jean? Sixty-three percent say they prefer quality to fashion, and when asked what characteristics are important for quality, 46 percent said fit or style; 30 percent mentioned durability or construction.

It's a definite, women shoppers say style and fit are consumers' number one priority in all clothing purchase decisions. As a merchant, please let this thought sink in as you go to market. Forget trying to find the most outrageous new look and the lowest prices. Select a good quality garment with style and great fit. Perhaps you will have at last answered the question - what do women really want? Nah...but you might at least have something they might like.

Another recent survey by Yanhkelovich Partners, Inc. for Lee Jeans and MARIE CLAIRE magazine, found that in the new corporate America, 84% of all women are allowed to wear casual clothing to work at least one day a week, while 48% could wear casual outfits every day. In 60% of the workplaces, women were allowed to wear denim. When asked questions about this casual lifestyle, the women answered:

> 42% said it makes them feel more productive at work.
>
> 98% said it is easier to pull together outfits for work.
>
> 93% said it saves them money on their work clothes.

Why Shoppers Leave Your Store Empty Handed

Why would a woman, intent on buying a new pair of pants, leave a store empty-handed? Every store owner in America would like to hear that answer. Lifestyle Monitor, a publication of Cotton, Inc. conducted a survey to find out exactly what customers today thought about their shopping experiences. They offered respondents 10 excuses for not buying apparel, and asked if they agreed or disagreed. The results found a significant number of women are not finding merchandise in their size, style or favorite colors.

This litany of potential excuses indicates that the merchandise they are finding does not meet their needs, and they have to spend too much time searching for what they like and need. And, for those shoppers looking for fashion direction, 56% said they get their clothing ideas from store displays or from window shopping. 16% said they got their ideas from sales people. (What a sad commentary this is on the state of sales asociates and customer service in our retail environment today.)

Lifestyle Monitor Survey Results

1. Current styles do not flatter my shape.................49%

2. Not as interested in clothes anymore...................47%

3. Rather spend money on other things...................46%

4. I'm afraid it'll be marked down soon...................44%

5. Can't find my size in clothes I like.......................41%

6. I don't have time to shop for clothes..................41%

7. Current styles are boring....................................35%

8. Merchandise is too spread out in stores,
    Too difficult to co-ordinate wardrobes................32%

9. The colors I like are not available.......................29%

10. I have too many clothes, I don't to shop *..........28%

* I find it very interesting that although 28% say they have enough clothes, that leaves 72% of all females who must currently **not** have all the clothes they want. They go into stores with the intent to buy, and will seek out stores that recognize their needs and perferences. They look for stores that offer good customer service. If there are sales associates who are educated to provide direction through the apparel maze, more shoppers will triumphantly exit the door with an outfit or two. Let's start fulfilling shopper's dreams and filling their shopping bags!

What Do Your Customers
F-E-A-R ?

They'll appear inferior or unintelligent. Symptoms of this fear are either aggressive, defensive, or shy behavior. Since people don't like the discomfort that this fear brings, they probably won't give you a second chance to sell them.

SOLUTION:Try to adjust the customer's behavior. Tone down your voice and gestures. Concentrate on sounding friendly and natural, so that clients can hear the warmth in your voice and/or see your smile. Avoid speaking in industry terms which the average person won't understand.

They might offend you. Studies show that people feel compelled to agree in sales situations, even though they disagree. Additionally to save time, they might not tell you everything you need to know.

SOLUTION:Make sure that you come across as a patient, good listener. Encourage them to speak by asking questions. Make agreement statements and gestures as they are speaking.

You won't understand their needs. Nobody likes to be sold something they later regret buying, because they have no need for it. Usually people who have this paranoia, have had a bad experience before.

SOLUTION: Get all of the information from your customer that you need to assess what they are hoping to gain from your service. Make customers feel at ease, by explaining that you have no intention of pressuring them.

They'll be sold something they can't afford. These people are the ones who crinkle their foreheads when cost is mentioned. They'll either be extremely quiet for the rest of the conversation or act indignantly & tell you *"You're dreaming if you think I'll pay that much!"*

SOLUTION: Don't get in a fighting match. Listen carefully to their financial concerns. Explain that although you understand their concerns, the benefits outweigh the costs. Define how those benefits apply to them. Tell them that the decision is theirs and that you don't want to consider it, if they are not completely satisfied and pleased.

You might waste their time. Symptoms of this fear are impatience, abruptness, and sometimes rudeness. Ironically these people are usually ones who can't manage their own time. Remember, personal time is important to everyone...including you.

SOLUTION:Let customers know that you respect their time. Ask if you may summarize your product and address their concerns efficiently. Avoid small talk if they don't want it.

Promises from you won't be honored. New customers are often hesitant to take the word of a stranger, These fears may be justified from a bad experience they had with one or more of your competitors.

SOLUTION:Always fulfill your promises to customers.

Follow the rules, and who knows, you might just get a ***REPUTATION!.***

Guarantee a Return Visit and PURCHASE

Ever wonder why people always seem to return to the same restaurants, the same grocery markets, the same gift shops, the same clothing stores? Do you think it's because those establishments have the best products, the best prices, the best location? Possibly, but....#1 on the list for most shoppers is comfort, familiarity, and a feeling of good will. In other words, they are looking for someone to be nice to them.

Yes, they'll drive out of the way to the place where people smile. They'll pay a little more money to the person who remembers their name, and they'll stay longer and come more often to the place where they feel the most comfortable. So pull out the chair, open a soda, and extend a welcoming hand and a friendly smile. Let's start selling.

The book, "Moods and Shopping Behavior" published by Management Horizons says, *"Appealing retail environments have a positive impact on customers, increasing the chances that they will purchase an item, but pleasant sales associates have the greatest effect on the moods and behavior of shoppers."*

Here is a checklist to improve your retail environment:

- Comfortable levels of lighting that are neither too bright or too dim
- Clothing displays set up to help customers co-ordinate outfits
- Uncluttered store layouts that eliminate the feeling of claustrophobia
- Signs that clearly tell customers where to find merchandise
- Music that compliments store image
- Soft interior colors
- Places to sit and rest
- Refreshements, such as soda or coffee
- Customer restrooms that are clean and attractive

All of the above basics can be easily implemented by a retail store owner. The cost and the time involved is minimal. What a store owner or manager can not always do is control what side of the bed your employee gets up on! There is no specific checklist for that, but please, spend your time and money on sales training. Too often we hire our neighbor's daughter and put her out on the sales floor the first day she shows up. This is not a sales associate; this is something taking up space and possibly running off your customers.

Carefully select and hire sales people who represent the image of your business and who believe in your personal philosophy that the customer comes first! Then, send them to seminars. Make available books for them to read. Rent videos on sales training and wardrobing. Make these people your ambassadors of goodwill.

A beautiful setting is wonderful; all the display and visual extras are fantastic and important, but first and foremost in creating a regular customer is courtesy. Make them feel at home with a big friendly welcoming smile and send them off with a warm, sincere thank you. This guarantees a profitable return visit!

Selling to the Senior Markets

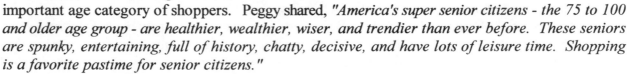

When I spoke at the Dallas Gift Super Show, I met Peggy Trees, the manager of the Lemon Tree Gift Shop in Northern Virginia who shared with me the following useful information about dealing with today's senior citizens.

Peggy's shop is located in a retirement community and I found it fascinating to learn how she markets to this important age category of shoppers. Peggy shared, *"America's super senior citizens - the 75 to 100 and older age group - are healthier, wealthier, wiser, and trendier than ever before. These seniors are spunky, entertaining, full of history, chatty, decisive, and have lots of leisure time. Shopping is a favorite pastime for senior citizens."*

In this day and age, seniors across the board, regardless of their background, are increasingly showing more dynamic ageless behavior, and retailers report that seniors are seeking fashion and upscale styles at reasonable prices. They are not limited by their age in styles, fabrics or cut.

Seniors invariably like products that are safe, easy, and efficient to use. Many prefer products, as do their younger counterparts. with environmental benefits such as recyclable materials. They favor products with guarantees and warranties, and they expect to be warned, before purchasing, about return policies and procedures. Open, accessible packaging is also a high priority. Seniors are proving to be no more or less brand loyal than young shoppers.

Seniors are enthusiastic gift-givers. First and foremost, they love to give gifts to grandchildren and great-grandchildren. Estimates are that 70 percent of those over age 80 are grandparents, having an average of five grandchildren 18 years or older, and great-grandchildren with an average age of five. The frequency of gift giving is three times a year, choosing from the celebrations of birthday, Christmas, graduation, wedding, or christening, In addition to giving gifts to grandchildren and great-grandchildren those over 80 are thoughtful givers to their own children and friends.

Nationwide almost 75 percent of elderly parents live within 25 miles of adult offspring and they see grandchildren and great-grandchildren often. They enjoy having goodies on hand to reward and treat.

Retailers note that senior's gift tastes run toward the traditional, preferring durable quality items instead of novelty and trend products. Seniors favor greeting cards, stationery, jewelry, collectable figurines such as bird and flowers, picture frames, and small decorative accessories. Even with a fixed pension, many seniors supplement their income with stock dividends and interest on saving accounts or C.D.'s. They do not hesitate to spend money on their gifts.

Quality service and salesmanship are sure ways to win the senior shopper. Seniors grew up with personalized service, especially in small towns, and they gravitate toward the stores that create that same *"tender loving care"* atmosphere. They relate to polite, educated salespeople who can locate and demonstrate products and who listen to their customer's complaints and needs. They appreciate and remember the sales person who takes the extra time to a read a greeting card verse, fill in a check, carry out a package, or offer suggestions. Seniors also tend to trust older sales people.

Don't forget this segment of society. It could mean money in the bank!

This is something you need to copy and post on the bulletin board in your employee area, stock room, etc. Encourage your staff to read this, memorize it and live it!

Who's the Boss?

There is only one boss, and whether a person shines shoes for a living or heads up the biggest corporation in the world, *the boss* remains the same. It's the CUSTOMER. The customer is the person who pays everyone's salary and decides whether a business is going to succeed or fail. And *"the boss"* doesn't care if a business has been around for 100 years.

The minute you start treating *the boss* badly, *the boss* will put you out of business. *The boss* (the customer) has bought you and will buy you everything you have or will have - your clothes, your home, your car, your vacations, your children's education. *The boss* pays all your bills, and pays in exact proportion to the way you treat him/her.

The person who works inside a big office building or plant might think he/she works for the company that writes the checks, but that's not true. They are working for *the boss* who buys the product at the end of the line. In fact, the customer will fire everyone in the company from the president down. And can do it simply by spending their money elsewhere.

Some of the largest companies that have had flourishing businesses in the past, are no longer in existence. They couldn't or didn't continue to satisfy the customer. They forgot who _the boss_ really is.

More Than Just A Sale

by Lynne Schwabe

Customers often buy because there is something more involved in their relationship than a product or service. Customers appreciate being appreciated. When salespeople make referrals on behalf of customers, recognize their achievements in conversations and in letters and cards, they are communicating to clients that they are appreciated as people, not just as an account.

One salesperson at a small store in West Virginia keeps notes on service providers that customers rave about. Consequently, when a customer mentions that they are redoing a bathroom, this clever sales person is able to say something like, *"Many of my customers have used Smith's Contracting. I understand they do the highest quality work and are quite reasonably priced."*

By becoming someone *in the know*, this sales person strengthened her relationships with customers. And, if in the course of discussing grout, the sales person happened to mention a new jacket that she thought the customer would like, that worked well, too!

Some salespeople, in fact, have become so good at creating relationships that their customers even consult them when they are buying clothing from other stores. Instead of being miffed that the customer is shopping somewhere else, these sales people turn their interactions into a chance to make more sales.

"When you get it all put together, stop by to show me. I think I have a wonderful topper that will look great over it!"

Here are some examples of what customers might appreciated hearing:

"The feature article in The New York Times *is about you. Your achievements in the industry are legendary."*

"Many of my customers are also business owners. I'm sure a lot of them would be interested in learning about the services your firm provides."

"Would it be all right to mention your company's products when my clients ask me about where they can find something like this?"

"Just wanted to congratulate you on your selection as Business Woman of the Year. Would you be willing to come by our office sometime and give an informal speech about how you succeeded in a very competitive industry? Many of the young women in our company could benefit from your insights."

"I'm just starting out in sales. Do you think it would be a good idea to focus on the successful business owners in your industry?"

"When is the best time of the year to contact people in your industry?"

"There are hundred of ways that a sales person could attempt to market to you. Tell me how you would like to be approached. In other words, do you prefer to be telephoned, paid a personal visit via a cold calla t your office or contacted by mail? Tell me what you would prefer - you have an opportunity to design a tailor made sales approach, just for you."

The Advertising Advantage

According to Webster's Dictionary, the term *advertising* means to "call attention to in order to sell" or "mention in a boastful manner," or "to inform and educate." Do you have an advertising campaign for your gift shop or specialty store that achieves these objections? Have you created a one year public relations plan for attracting new shoppers and enticing back old customers while still maintaining an advertising budget between 4 to 7 % of your annual sales volume? Having the most wonderful merchandise in a gorgeous setting does absolutely no good if you haven't sent out an invitation for shoppers to come see.

When deciding how to lure in prospective customers, think about what it takes to makeup a successful ad:

(1) Look for a response. What action do you want from the reader or listener? Is it a one-day event and they must come in today? Does the offer run out on a deadline date? Is your ad for image, asking them to think about how up-to-date or modern you are? Is there a special item that they must have NOW? Will this collectible fly out on first notice? Is it a limited edition or exclusive only to you in the area? Choose the correct medium and wording to achieve the response you desire. Merchants throughout Canada and the U.S. have created beanie frenzies on a regular basis just by making the right announcements in the right mediums about the Ty Beanie Babies. You are seeking this type of response on your advertising. Put thought into each word, remembering every letter means money - not only the cost of the ad, but the business you will be getting from using the right words.

(2) Make them *feel* the ad. Invoke an emotion such as love, humor, fear or fright by involving the customer's feelings. Aim for the heart, the soul or even the stomach by offering refreshments. *"You're gonna love this!"* Or perhaps *"Don't lose out on the* thrill *of a lifetime!"* Or *"You'll be the perfect hostess with this new place setting."* Or *"Don't miss out on the 10th piece of the 12 piece set. Serious Collector Alert - valuables going fast!"* Or *"Imagine yourself dancing on air in a dress from* _____ _____." The advertisement should fit the inventory and take aim at the right customer. Personalize to fit your product. Anytime you can tug at the heartstrings, you can make a sale. Why do you think so many companies use cuddly little animals or babies in their advertising? What does a tyke in a diaper have to do with selling tires in the rain? A lot, it makes parents think and then they buy new tires to protect their loved ones.

(3) Surprise 'em! People are bombarded with so many ad messages, try to make yours memorable. Think of Michael Jordan grabbing that rim 300 feet off the ground or that kid getting stuffed into the Pepsi bottle. Didn't that surprise you enough to remember those ads? OK, so you're not Nike - but you can be different and you can make your ads memorable in your own unique fashion to fit your personality. It's an "anything goes world." Joe Camel helped convince a generation to start smoking. Who would have ever imagined frogs selling Budweiser Beer and then being upstaged by Iguanas?

I was once told a humorous advertising story about old general store in Montana. It seems the buyer was way over bought in red flannel shirts and finally broke down and decided to run an ad marking them to half-price. His ad drew more attention than any he ever ran in the store's 50 year history. Not because the shirts were such a great deal at half-price but because he left out the letter R in the word shirt ! People did come into the store and respond, mostly with laughter.

(4) Hit the target! Make sure your ad involves your customer. This will be easy if you have done surveys and created target market lists of your customers. Throughout this book I talk about demographics and age categories. This is the best way to determine who your customer is and what they are looking for in products to buy. Sample ad statements: *"Body lotions for the woman who wants her skin to be it's smoothest,"* or *"Candles to compliment your warm and cozy home."* or *"Gourmet chocolates for lips with discriminating taste"* or *"Does your home need a total new look at a very low price?"* The customer needs to feel it was aimed straight at them, as if to say, *"Hey,they're talking about me These people understand ME. They want me as a customer."* People tend to spend their money where they feel invited, comfortable, and needed, Everyone wants to "fit in" and more importantly - feel IMPORTANT.

By involving response, feeling, surprise, and actually aiming your message at your targeted customer, you will achieve a successful ad campaign, whether it's radio, television, newspaper or other print mediums. Remember to keep consistency in your advertising and your image. In those fleeting seconds make sure your customers can identify you, and your message which you have personalized especially for them!

Promotion & Advertising - The Name Game

Most specialty store owners enjoy buying, selling, displaying, etc. but hate the thought of planning a promotion or creating an ad campaign. Don't dread these tasks; they're easy. The secret to successful promotion and advertising is as simple as writing a grade school English paper. Before beginning, you to determine the (1) Who (2) What (3) Where (4) When and (5) Why.

Plan your promotion to target the WHO with the WHAT, WHEN and WHY in WHERE, (the medium in which you wish to advertise). There is a small resortwear shop in Miami Beach that uses their window as their medium to target passers-by offering a discount if the customer is named the today's special name on that particular day! (i.e. A sign in the window reads: TODAY IS MARILYN DAY!)

The WHO is the _passerby_: the WHAT is the _discount_; the WHEN is _today_: the WHY is the _name_; the WHERE is the _window!_ See, I told you this was easy, and it will work for pageant shops, formal wear stores, gift shops, pharmacies, beauty salons, and even children's boutiques. Everyone is proud of their name!

This store owner has found a very unique and creative way to draw customers in to purchase items. The entire promotion uses very little effort and even less money! Actually the only expense is a sign in the window and the discount given. This can be used as a weekly or daily promotion in any busy area. It will keep people coming by on a regular basis to check for their name. I recommend limiting the discount to one item only. I feel you would get the same response if it were one item or the entire sale, without having to give away the store in markdowns.

You may want to keep records on the most popular and most unusual names. If you want to fudge on the deal, you could call special people and tell them, *"Today is your name day!"* Make an advance list of everyone you *know* with a particular name and plan your promotion accordingly. *P.S. Don't tell anyone you did that. The crime is not in doing, but in telling!* You can guarantee those who got the discounts won't complain!

Recent surveys show that shoppers have gotten accustomed to making their purchases on sale. This is not entirely true of all merchandise categories, but every business from clothing to stuffed rabbits, gourmet coffee, and housewares has customers who come looking for the markdowns. Our customers like the thought of getting that little extra savings or that special something that everyone else didn't receive. Coupons, games, contests, and any other promotion that can put the fun back into shopping without depleting your pocketbook is a good way to increase your sales and your customer average. Every promotion should attract new and different shoppers. Whether you retain them as loyal customers will depend upon the service and merchandise you have to offer.

Learn to Toot Your Own Horn

When I present advertising and publicity programs across the country it is sometimes difficult to convince store owners that they need to *"Toot their own horn."* We were all raised by good parents who taught us it was impolite to brag and draw attention to ourselves. Forget that! Honey, you are now in show business, and it's time to start *"Showing Off!"*

The first thing you need to do is to establish yourself as a *"know it all"* in your field. Make people aware of who you are and what you do. I am going to list ways for you to become known in your community as an *"expert"* in your industry. I'll illustrate how to present your business as the leader by spotlighting your professional image. These are examples of activities, advertising, and promotions to establish this identity.

<u>Free of Inexpensive Ways to Toot</u>

(1) Press releases: *What* to say, *when*, *how* and to *who*! You know *why*!
(2) Visible community sponsorships: Charity, school, civic & volunteer
(3) Business changes: remodeling, new employees, retirements, promotions, New line of merchandise, special anniversary, big contest.
(4) Anything that is worthy - wonderful - or *WEIRD*!

SAMPLE PRESS RELEASE

Contact: Stu Store owner
713-555-7853

STU STORE OWNER ATTENDS PROFESSIONAL APPAREL MEET

Mr. Stu Store owner of Life World Apparel and Equipment of St. Louis, Missouri recently returned from San Antonio, Texas where he was one of fifty retailers from across the nation to attend the meeting of the Professional Apparel Association. Stu spent three days deep in the heart of Texas, home of the Alamo and enjoyed both networking with other store owners and attending education classes conducted by retail consultant and business author, T.J. Reid.

Stu invites you to drop the store and see the new and unique lines of apparel he has now gotten in the store and talk about his recent Texas experience. Come in today!

THIS PRESS RELEASE IS IDEAL FOR LOCAL NEWSPAPER BUSINESS SECTIONS AND TO SEND TO COMMUNITY SHOPPER PAPERS.

Experts put the *word on the street* that they are available to take part in community activities that involve or will support and promote their business. Here is a list of some simple easy things I used to do for my clothing and gift shop.

☆What Experts Do:
(1) Write columns for the newspaper.

I wrote columns for three different newspapers over the 20 years I was in business in Amite. (I'd get tired and quit for a year or so, then start over again.) Columns were entitled "Uptown-Downtown," and "What's Up in Amite" and "A Woman's Place." Each one basically just talked about what was going on in town, with special mentions of women's and school events, and of course, individuals. Customers loved to see their name in the paper and all comments were always complimentary. The newspapers were glad to have someone fill their space with good news and they were always accommodating in allowing me to mention new items or events at the store at no charge. One paper even traded my column for additional advertising space. Needless to say, I wrote really long columns to secure really big ads!

(2) Give seminars and shows for local groups.

There is some kind of meeting going on in your town every single day. Whether it's a Sunday School group, a Rotary regional convention or a PTA meeting, each one is looking for a program speaker - someone to educate and entertain their attendees. It could be you! Over my many years in the store I spoke to groups ranging from five to five hundred and made as much as $5,000 on one of those events. All I did was demonstrate merchandise from your store and invite the audience to "follow" me back. Usually, I distributed coupons for a discount to new customers or offered special door prize drawings to those who made purchases. However you do it, make it fun and informative - not just a sales pitch. Listeners know the difference and will be turned off if they think you are just there to raid their pocketbooks. Teach someone how to tie a scarf and they will decide they need to buy a new one show off their new found talent!

(3) Offer programs for tourists at hotels.

That $5,000 in meeting sales came from a Rotary convention program I gave at a local Holiday Inn. All these people were here from out-of-town to attend a regional meeting. The hotel needed a spouse program to keep the ladies entertained while the men had their sessions. My show was so much fun the women followed me in droves to my store. I even had a van pick up those who didn't have transportation. For the entire three days they were in town we were swamped with women spending money. Get in touch with the person at your local hotel that plans and sets up conventions and meetings. Make friends and be the lucky one they call.

(4) Host a radio talk-show (everybody's doing it!)

Ever wonder how some of those people get on the air? Because it's free! All you have to do in most cases is offer your services to the local station. Aren't you a fashion expert or an interior decorator or an expert on gourmet cooking? Whatever your field, volunteer to do a show about that topic. Give advice, ask for call-ins, and just talk. It's a sure fire way to stir up interest in you and your business. If they won't let you host a show, at least be a guest on somebody's time. Offer to give away freebies on the air - like t-shirts or discount coupons or gift certificates . . . . or. . . you think of what your audience would delight in.

(5) Do demonstrations or style shows at restaurants.

If you are a fashion shop, present the old tried and true style show. Have restaurant styling where models go through the room from table to table telling their outfits or just handing out cards with the store name. If you sell other items such as gourmet foods, do the old Sam's Wholesale routine - offer free samples to everyone you see. You can do this in a hair salon, a spa, a diet center, anywhere women pass and gather.

(6) Offer turn-down service & maps at hotels & inns.

I once met a lady who had the only clothing store in a very small town, but the community did have a local inn. The store owner paid the housekeeper to put out a peppermint each evening on the pillow along with an invitation to shop at her store. The letter read, *"While you are visiting our town, please take time to come by _____and shop. We offer a wide selection of _____ and would love to have your business. If you do not have a ride to the store, just call us at _____-and someone will pick you in minutes. Here is a $5.00 gift certificate to use on your first visit."* This store owner said she got at least three customers a week from this ad which certainly more than paid for the effort.

(7) Form relationships with other merchants.

Everybody needs friends, and your best ones should be the non-competitive businesses in your town. A referrals from another respected merchant is the advertisement you can ever receive. Customers pay attention when a retailer says something nice about another business. I often received referrals from the car dealership in town. Women would come in to have their car serviced and have an extra hour or so to kill. The Ford salesman once said, *"My wife loves to shop at T.J.'s. It's right up the street, would you like me to drop you off there while your car is being repaired? I'll pick you up as soon as we're finished,"* Of course the lady jumped at the chance to spend time in a nice clean clothing store as opposed to the greasy mechanic setting of the a garage. That one event became a regular occurrence and the beginning of a great relationship. I, of course, often gave him discounts and coupons for his wife. He deserved them; that was word-of-mouth advertising I could not afford to buy.

The same opportunities are open with every single business in town. Give lunch coupons to shoppers to visit a local deli. Offer free fresh roses from the florist with a $200 purchase; a discount at the hair salon with an hat or barrette purchase. There are so many different ways to cross-promote with your fellow store owners. Get together and work this out through your chamber of commerce. Exchange mail lists and send advertising packages together. It saves money and draws new customers.

(8) ADVERTISE by example every minute of the day!

If you are a fashion center, you better be well-dressed. If you sell household items, you better have a nicely appointed home. If you sell gourmet items, you better be the best cook in town...at least make people think you are. Remember, YOU are your business. Set the example for yourself and your employees. They represent you, too.

Experts Have IMAGE

What is IMAGE? According to Webster:

Im-age (im'ij) n. 1. A physical likeness or representation of a person or thing. 2. The appearance of an object. 3. An idea; a conception. 4. A representation of something previously conceived 5. A general *perception of a company*, especially when achieved by calculation for the purpose of goodwill. 6. To symbolize, typify or be construed as.

The key word in that interpretation is *"Perception."* It is wonderful if you are what you advertise yourself to be, but actually it is perception - what people actually perceive or believe that counts. There are many techniques used to promote the image of expertise and knowledge.

The first one is through constant visibility and deeds. This is achieved through press releases like the one I illustrated. Use a press release every time you attend a seminar or acquire additional knowledge or certification. Customers like to know you are well-informed and trained in your field. Frame those diplomas and awards and display them prominently on the walls near the checkout counter or in your office. This is not bragging; it is keeping the customer aware.

The key word in that paragraph was *"constant"*. Only by constantly repeating a pattern will you achieve your objective of making yourself well-known. Continually create good publicity and do good deeds that get noticed over and over again. Someone may miss this once, even twice but after a while everybody will be aware of what you are doing! Repetition causes people to read, react and respond.

☆ What Experts Use: LOGOS - SYMBOLS - GRAPHICS

Customers identify a company or a business through their logo, their giftwrap, their signage, etc. What have you established as the theme of your advertising? Does your logo automatically identify your product, your location, your service? Is there a continuity in your advertising, your store decor, your gift wrap, your packaging, your billboards and your window display?

Here is a list of some of America's most popular logos and symbols of well known established, and respected companies. Can you fill in the blank?

HALLMARK - _____
TY - _____
NIKE - _____
GREG NORMAN - _____
IZOD - _____
ROLEX - _____
RALPH LAUREN - _____
ELIZ. ARDEN - _____
LEVIS - _____
BLOOMINGDALEs - _____
TIFFANY - _____
CBS- _____NBC - _____ABC - _____

The answers are on the following page. See how many you identified. (Don't cheat!)

Some of the most recognized logos in America are:

(1) Hallmark uses a crown as its symbol. Through extensive and repetitive advertising they has convinced most Americans to send *only* a Hallmark greeting card, because the recipient will turn the card over and see the crown - an insurance that the giver cared enough to send the very best!

(2) TY, the parent company of Beanie Babies has hearts (❤) as tags. What a wonderful way to touch and warm the heart of every customer who touches some of these warm and fuzzy animals.

(3) Nike, home of the famous swoosh, is known to just about everyone on the planet. If you are ever in Chicago, take the opportunity to visit Nike Town on Michigan Avenue. This is a Mecca for tourists and a museum of how Nike does it all! It's an actually store, but it is also the story of Nike, displaying Michael Jordan's shoes, Tiger's golf clubs and Scottie's jersey. You'll note there are swooshs everywhere - even the door knobs are a swoosh!

(4) Greg Norman is the shark and it's sewn into every shirt and pair of golf slacks in his line. Everyone on the course recognizes that big straw hat with the wide band branded SHARK!

(5) Izod, another company whose shirts bear their symbol - the alligator.

(6) Rolex, the highest quality in watches has a high crested crown as an emblem.

(7) Ralph Lauren is so familiar for the polo pony and rider crest.

(8) Elizabeth Arden has the red door.

(9) Levis shows off their red tab tag.

(10) Bloomingdale's is known for their brown shopping bag.

(11) Tiffany is famous for their blue box.

(12) The symbol of CBS is an eye.

(13) The symbol of NBC is a peacock.

(14) ABC has no logo or symbol. Maybe that's why they're # 3.

Use your logo in giveaway items such as t-shirts, tote bags, coupons, calendars, golf balls, litter bags, magnets, emery boards, and mouse pads.

VERY IMPORTANT WORDS OF ADVICE: Create your image and stick to it - follow through with each detail. The word is, I repeat, *CONTINUITY!*

When you open your mail box each morning, I do not have to point out to you that despite the rising cost of postage. direct mail today is at it's highest volume ever in history. More and more small businesses are realizing it is not only the easiest but also the most economical way to reach their target customer. Direct mail is a one-on-one medium in which a business attempts to deliver a message of interest to a customer who has a need for the item. It doesn't matter what type of business you have. It doesn't matter whether you use a letter, a postcard or a package.

The following are six fundamental keys for direct mail success that you must adhere to:

(1) THE RIGHT LIST

The right list is as critical to the success of your mailing as the offer or the product or service itself. As an example, you can mail miniature garden catalogues all day long to condo dwellers and not get much response. But if you discover a list of condo dwellers who subscribe to a miniature gardening magazine, then you have an almost guaranteed winner.

You can't choose the right list unless you have a clear definition of who your target audience is. When considering direct mail, the first question to ask is *"Who is the primary target audience,"* and then work with a list researcher to get as specific as possible so you can purchase or find lists effectively. In most areas you can secure your church membership list, the local school PTA lists, the Chamber of Commerce membership lists, new residents list, etc. There are also many local non-competitive merchants who would jump at the chance of sharing their list in return for yours.

(2) THE RIGHT PRODUCT OR SERVICE

You wouldn't put a Snapper Lawn Mower or a John Deere tractor dealership in downtown New York City, but you would put a Rolls Royce or Cadillac dealership. Julian Simon, a noted speaker on direct mail has the theory that the right product is one that's being successfully advertised repeatedly over an extended period of time. The general rule is that if you've seen it in the mail more than once then it's probably safe. Witness offers for donations and contributions to charities and the many sweepstakes offers. The key is offering the target audience a product they have a desire and need for. If you're a retailer that may be tracking your customers by what they buy and then offering a sale on that certain item to that certain customer, you're an expert! If you aren't using this data in that manner, you're losing money!

(3) THE RIGHT OFFER

The offer is considered by many to be as important as the list. Without the right offer, the list and even the product become meaningless. As a comparison, two companies recently mailed an offering for the same thing to the same list: One was from a company offering to come out and inspect computer systems that were in a building that had experienced a massive power surge. This was free of charge if you would sit and listen to a five minute pitch about insurance for your computer system. The other direct mail was a $69.95 special to come out and check your system for problems. The first company took the long range approach and gained entry to almost every office in the building, and undoubtedly sold many service contracts that will pay off for years to come. The other company . . . they're still waiting for the phone to ring!

(4) THE RIGHT FORMAT

What's the difference between mailing and solicitation for a newsletter in a nine by twelve envelope or sending a postcard? The answer is the 9X12 package has been proven over and over again to be the most successful package for a newsletter solicitation because a postcard does not allow enough room to properly present an offer. On the other hand, to offer a special price on swimsuits for one day, a single postcard is more than sufficient and is easy to read and attract attention. Take time to read and research all the different mail offers you receive each week. Find the ones that YOU prefer and that can apply to your business.

Birthday cards and thank you cards work better as post cards, not as cards in envelopes. The easier it is for the message to be read, the better. Also post cards tend to end up on the refrigerator as a reminder.

(5) THE RIGHT TESTS

Results are the true hallmark of direct marketing. There are so many things that can go wrong with a campaign, yet due to budget restraints or lack of belief, very few mailers are willing to test one package against another. Tests can be as simple as two competing offers in exactly the same package or as complex as two separate distinct mailings. Whatever you choose, remember the thing to test first is the offer, then change other elements around that. Often an offer at $99.00 will draw many more results than one at $100 - just because the offer is *"less than $100."* A *"Buy One - Get One FREE"* sounds much better than *"Half-Price"* or *"Two for the Price of One."* There are certain words that work. **Free**, of course is #1!

(6) THE RIGHT ANALYSIS

This is where many people fail. They go through the steps flawlessly but fail to follow through and track the progress of the campaign, whether it's calculating response rates, break-even points, or inquiries as opposed to actual purchases.. One of the reasons many mailing companies and even ad agencies don't do this or recommend this to their clients is fear. They are afraid that if a mailing doesn't perform properly they'll lose the account. If you are doing this yourself, you sometimes are afraid to admit that the mailer you <u>loved</u> was just a pretty piece of fluff rather than an effective profit generator.

You must also realize that each direct mailing will not always pay for itself, but each one will lead to the future success of others and the recognition factor of your business. It's important to generate a repeat buyer who will visit and purchase again and again generating revenue for years to come.

And direct mail does just that . . . successfully!

What is Direct Mail?

Direct Mail can be any of the following items:

✍1. A Letter

✍2. A Postcard

✍3. A Brochure

✍4. A Catalog

✍5. Newsletter

✍6. A Fax

✍7. An E-Mail

which are targeted to a potential customer to gain business.

Any direct mail piece should be written to introduce and identify the store or product. It should grab the reader's immediate attention, and it should create an urgency to respond. Include a return coupon or dept. #, or some identification to analyze the success of your campaign. Figure cost of direct mail piece sent (creation, printing, mailing). Calculate number of responses and total of sales per response. When determining if the mailing was a success, consider new additions to your customer mailing list, and the value of community goodwill and image creation.

Direct mail is written to motivate a customer to buy. Does your product relate to any of the following basic motivators of life?

(1) Food & Shelter - the physiological needs for sustaining life

(2) Safety & security

(3) Social acceptance, friendship, belonging to a group

(4) Ego needs, esteem and status

(5) Self-actualization or self-fulfillment - making a contribution to humanity

I am sure your items fit in there somewhere. Here are motivators you can apply to direct mail:

Exclusivity	Money(greed)	Pride of ownership
Security	Status	Peer Pressure & acceptance
Belonging	Self-improvement	Beauty and Sexual Attraction
Family Love	Power Prestige	Comfort & Health
Recognition	Praise - Advantage	Pity or Pleasure

Most people are either looking for these things, or in fear of losing them. Either way, you have touched the right *hot button* for grabbing the customer's attention. You got it - they need it, that's about as direct as you get.

25 Tips to Great Direct Mail:

1. Dollar for Dollar, nothing returns as much to your business as direct mail.
2. Your customer list will return 2 to 10 response as much as a rented list.
3. Renting a list for use for 1 year is usually only double the cost of a single use.
4. Mail postcards first class. It cleans your list at no extra cost.
5. Average delivery for 3rd class mail is <u>ten</u> days! First class is 3 days.
6. Mail ALL names on your list *at least* 4 times a year.
7. Mail *"Best Customer List"* every six weeks!
8. On an good offer you'll receive 90% of your response in the first three days.
9. Check with the post office *before* your mailings to see if it fits the rules.
10. What's first read? THE HEADLINE.
11. What's second read? THE P. S.
12. Ask *"Is this name and address correct?"* Get the reader involved.
13. The more you use the word **"YOU"** - the greater the response.
14. Customers buy confidence. Offer a BIG easy to read GUARANTEE!
15. Watch the size of mailers: *Too big* equals too much postage.
16. The more you tell - the more you sell. Put as much in the envelope as you can !
17. Compare costs: Sending 1,000 letters first class is only about $100 more than sending 3rd class. They are delivered faster and they're delivered!
18. Success is not *"cost per unit mailed."* Success is *"cost per sale!"*
19. More than half your future business comes from your present customers.
20. Multiple mailings are more effective than single mailings.
21. Try *"piggy backing"* with non-competitive businesses. Cuts printing and postage costs.
22. Personal copy is more important than personalized copy. Show warmth, friendship.
23. The list is the most important factor in a mailing.
24. The most powerful word in the English Language is **"FREE!"**
25. Back up your promises with action when they arrive at the store.

DIRECT MAIL is made up of three parts:

The list is responsible for 40% of your success.

The offer is responsible for 40% of your success.

The creative is responsible for 20% of your success.

Henderson's Hints - An Invitation that Brings in Sales!

One of my dearest store friends is Beth Henderson, a third generation retailer from Henderson's Department Store in Sycamore, Illinois. She is constantly coming up with something and different, and best yet - profitable.

Because she is a very civic minded person, Beth is always trying to cross-promote and work with her local merchants and chamber to create benefits for all downtown merchants. The invitation below is one she sent to please the local business owners and their employees. It's a special early morning invitation to visit her store and save. Beth said even if a business has only four or five employees it is still worth it for for her business to open early and provide the juice and bagels. It helps to build her mailing list and customer base. What a wonderful idea to get new people excited over your store!

To: Samantha Dailey at First National Bank
From: Beth Willey at Henderson's
Re: A Special Invitation

I would like to invite you and your entire staff to Henderson's on the weekday morning of your choice from 7:30 AM to 9:00 AM for

BREAKFAST....BARGAINS.....and BANTER!

Breakfast, Bargains, and Banter is a new program we are offering to local businesses, who can in turn, offer this to all of their employees. On the selected date, your staff would have our entire store to themselves for a closed door shopping experience. Henderson's will provide a free continental breakfast for your staff, personalized service, and a discount of 20% off the lowest marked price of all sale and regular priced merchandise throughout our store.

If this sounds like a morning your staff would enjoy, give me a call and we can set a date. This is all free of charge...all you have to do is tell your employees and bring them on the date we agree upon....We look forward to your visit!

P.S. We have done this with our own staff and Kar-Fre Flowers...they loved it! They found it's fun to have the whole store to themselves...and the fun we had after shopping during "show and tell" was a great team building experience.

BETH WILLEY

HENDERSON'S DEPARTMENT STORE - 815-895-4535

Planning That Special Event?
Ask Yourself These Questions

A Sale is not a *special event*; a promotion is not a *special event*. A *special event* is planned for the entertainment, encouragement, education, excitement and of course, enticement of customers. It does not have *selling* as it's primary purpose. It is an activity which should create goodwill and *future* profits. (See the key word "profits" is still definitely part of the overall plan. You are doing this to make money - later.)

There are many categories of events to choose from

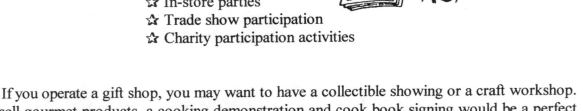

☆ Style Shows
☆ Trunk Shows
☆ Artist's Signings
☆ Women's Seminars
☆ Author Book Signings
☆ In-store parties
☆ Trade show participation
☆ Charity participation activities

If you operate a gift shop, you may want to have a collectible showing or a craft workshop. If you sell gourmet products, a cooking demonstration and cook book signing would be a perfect event. If housewares and home accessories are your category, invite a well known interior decorator to speak to your customers. There is no end to the numerous ideas that could be generated for every business imaginable.

First things first. In planning, think about those words I like to use when talking about advertising - the When - Where - Why - What - and for Who theory. Even before those words, the #1 major consideration is *"How Much?"* What budget do you have, and what results will this eventually bring to the store? What is the time frame of the event - the season - the day - the time?

WHAT is the primary goal? What do you expect to accomplish with this event? Are you trying to reward present and old customers? Are you looking to attract new customers? Do you wish to be perceived as a kind, upstanding, generous contributing member of the community? Are you attempting to educate customers about clothing, health, cooking, fitness, shopping, or just women, in general? Are you trying to spotlight your products, a particular line, a certain department, your facility, your staff or your store as a whole?

After we determine the what, the WHERE becomes a big factor. Is it in-store or off the premises? If it is outside the store, then it must appeal to customers *and* fit your image. Are your shoppers country club types or would they prefer the local Moose Lodge? The location should be easily accessible to all attendees and provide adequate and safe parking. Is the site already set up with tables and chairs, music and microphones? Will there be additional decorations required? Will you serve refreshments? Can it be catered or will you have to bring in the food? How much will this cot in money, and in additional work for staff to use this facility? Have you already gotten exhausted from all these questions and decided not to have any *special event* after all? Don't give up. I promise it's not as difficult as it sounds.

I know a store who had a dinner style show for 100 customers. She asked 10 of her friends to each volunteer to set up tables of eight. Each person was totally in charge of their table, using their own favorite china, tablecloths, floral centerpiece, and silverware. The room was so beautifully decorated - each table was a special scene to itself. The food was an easily arranged buffet of casserole with side salad, mixed vegetables and a roll. See how simple - how different - how fun. If serving a meal sounds too complicated, just opt for wine and cheese or brown bag lunches or even punch and cookies.

Advertising any type of *special event* can be very costly. If you can involve a local charity or social group as a co-sponsor, your newspaper and media coverage can all be free of charge, and easy to obtain. They will seldom say no to a charity organization. Everybody wants to lend a helping hand if profits are going for a worthy cause. Look around for a group who represents a cause you feel sincere about. There are thousands of them out there needing assistance. Ask your better customers for their charity choices. A good customer with a great cause is your best insurance for a successful charity function. (She'll bring *all* her friends!)

Promoting the Event

To advertise, use fliers that you can have printed locally, and distributed through your store and other places where women shop or gather. Use your mailing list to send these invitations; enlist school children to hand out fliers; barter free tickets with your radio station and trade out tickets for talk time about the *special event* and it's importance to the community.

Tickets? Yes, I would charge. Any event that is free appears to be worth what it costs. Women expect to pay for a worthwhile evening. Whether it is a speaker or fashion show or demonstration, you need an approximate attendance figure. By advance ticket sales you will have an idea of how many to expect. Otherwise, there is no way to plan for seating or refreshments. By charging admission, the event becomes important - something to look forward to. Women will buy tickets in groups; use a *"fun girls night out"* approach. Most stores offer rebates on tickets - i.e. a $5.00 coupon off any item in the store if the attendee brings in the ticket stub within a week.

Door prizes? Yes, but very few. The event itself is the important activity, and they are already there. Save the door prizes for later when the customers bring their ticket stubs back into the store. Ask everyone to drop their ticket stubs at the store by the weekend and they will be eligible for a special drawing. This way you will have them attend the event AND come into the store.

Follow-up any event with a thank you note. You should ask each person who attends to register. (Remember, you are promising door prizes later so they'll be glad to give you their name and address for a chance to win a $100 gift certificate!) A week following the event, send each attendee a letter of thanks, expressing your gratitude and inviting them to drop by. This would be a perfect time to mention some new item or some specific item that was not promoted during the *special event*. It's always recommended to keep providing customers with new and unique items and exciting information and promotions. This is how a loyal customer relationship is built.

Great Promotional Ideas

Here are six to consider from Lynne Schwabe:

The Great Ice Caper: One merchant bought a large quantity of inexpensive cubic zirconia - enough for one for each of his good customers. He also bought one small real diamond. He then invited his most valuable customers to a party at the store to celebrate The Great Ice Caper. As the customers entered the store, they were handed an ice cube in which a zirconia or the real diamond was frozen. Customers had to wait while the ice melted to see who got what (there was a jeweler on hand to verify the stones) and they shopped while they waited. Customers' finding zirconia received 25% off their purchases, but the customer who found the diamond got to keep it. Everyone had a great time and the store made sales far in excess of the original investment. Customers are still talking!

I'll Give You $10: to come to my party. One retailer in Colorado invited all his customers to a party at the store, promising to give each $10 for attending. As customers walked in the door, each was handed a crisp ten dollar bill. How much did the store spend? $3,000 ! How much did they make? $22,000! *"I never was so scared in all my life,"* the owner said. *"But the customers loved it and we all had a wonderful time."*

$25 Thank You For Shopping: Each year a store in West Virginia sends a $25 gift certificate to all its charge customers as a "thank you" gift. The certificates are mailed early in November so that they are an incentive for Christmas shopping. Certificates are good on purchases of $100 and above and cannot be accepted as payment on account. Up to as many as 80 percent of its customers redeems the gift certificate each year.

Kareoke Party: One store in Colorado had a Kareoke contest for three weekends running. They set up Kareoke equipment in the store, encouraged customers and passersby to enter and had a local radio personality pick the winners. *"This turned out to be a huge party,"* the store owner said. *"We had more traffic than we've ever had, sold more merchandise. And got free publicity in the paper and on the radio for three weeks running. Customers are still talking about it."*

While We Were Closed: A store that was located next to one of the town's most popular restaurants was frustrated because the restaurant's customers were walking by the store after hours. To take advantage of the traffic, the store filmed an "infomercial" on its merchandise, put it in the front window, and turn it when they leave the store each night. They change the video once a month. This simple solution increased their business by 25 percent.

Whole Town Promotion: In one small town that is fighting the encroachment of Big Box retailers, the merchants are targeting small meeting planners, bus tours and corporate meeting planners and offering coupons for discounts in local shops as an incentive for those groups coming to the area. The program has not only increased the number of small meeting booking in the region, but it has spun off into a full-fledged spouse event shopping program, which brings desirable couples to town on a regular basis.

Getting customers in the door is never easy, but there is no reason that both customers and retailers can't have a little fun while trying. See what creative ideas you can come up with!

Spring Promotions
By Lynne Schwabe

Boost your Spring profits by getting customers egg-cited about Easter events in your store. Give them a reason to shop by making your store someplace that's fun to visit, a destination where they can make all their Spring purchases.

By partnering with a local florist, you can create a floral atmosphere on a shoestring in your store. Let your local florist provide the blooms and transform your windows into gardens that will be the perfect backdrop for your Spring fashions. You take care of advertising, giving the florist credit in both the ads and in your windows. A small potted plant makes a lovely and living gift-with-purchase.

Instead of an Easter egg hunt, let your customers look for something a little different and have fun doing it. One retailer hid fortune cookies-some containing news of gifts, gift certificates and coupons- throughout his store for customers to find. The gifted cookie personalizes original or chocolate-covered fortune cookies ($25-$45 for 60 cookies with 10 different messages-call Linda Atkinson-**(206)525-6335**).

Honor outstanding volunteers in your community. Distribute entry forms in the store and get publicity through local newspapers, asking the public to submit nominees and reasons why they should be honored. A panel of local dignitaries can judge the event. Once the 10 winners have been selected, contact them to be sure they will accept the framed award. Make the presentation the weekend before Easter at a black-tie award dinner and dance at a local hotel. Proceeds from admission should be donated to charitable organizations selected by the award winners.

Events like these are often sellouts because everyone wants to show support for the good cause. They also give your customers an occasion to dress up, which can boost your formal wear sales prior to the event. At each award dinner table setting, leave a store gift certificate for $25, good toward a purchase of $100 or more.

For creative and well-rounded direct-mail marketing program ideas contact Denny Nisch at Palmer Marketing - **(800)654-1511**. This is a fantastic company for marketing needs.

Other gift-with-purchase ideas include:

* Premiums ranging from garden books and cookbooks to CD's and tapes, typically 60% below retail. Call Debbie Robinson - **(317) 228-1145**

* "Fly-Free America" travel premiums in the form of airline tickets to worldwide destinations at prices ranging from $4-$14 per pair. The only restriction is that travelers stay at stipulated hotels or resorts and pay the published room rates. Minimum 100 tickets. Call Bridgette Wagner - **(407) 362-6707.**

* Tote All, it folds like a bag but works like a box. Terrific incentive or gift-with-purchase for shoppers. The company minimum is two cases (36 pieces) at $5.50 per bag. Call Roy Gilbert - **(800) 638-3201.**

Tourists are Here. Sell!

Regardless of whether or not you are in a hot bed of popular tourism or some small out of the way country town, summertime always brings vacationers in from out-of-town, even if it's just Susie's second cousin from Detroit. Don't ever underestimate your city - there are strangers there in the summer months. Figure out how to get their business, because as I've reported again and again, a vacationer's top activity is shopping. They came to spend - help them succeed!

The Friend of a Friend Method:
Encourage your regular customers to bring in family and friends who are visiting. Offer a discount or a special to shoppers with an out-of-state driver's license or give them a small memento from your store (t-shirt, etc.). Reward your good friends and customers who do bring in their summer referrals. It doesn't have to be much, but a thank you is remembered, appreciated, and the effort will be repeated.

Use of Billboard Space:
If you're near a major highway, use billboards to advertise your specialty. Encourage travelers to stop in for fashion and fun. A free glass of cool lemonade may be just the teaser they need to pull off at your exit sign.

Welcome to our City:
Form a relationship with local hotels, restaurants, service stations - anywhere that out-of-towners might stop. Leave brochures on the counters. Promote yourself everywhere possible, and make sure the people in your community know *who you are and where you are,* so they can recommend you to visitors who ask!

Where Ya From?
Why not put up a map by the register and put a push pin in for each out-of-area visitor during the summer months? You'll see where your customers are coming from. It is a great conversation starter when strangers come in, and you'll find people who stop to talk, also stop to shop. If they are regular vacationers to your area, put them on your mailing list and send them a note prior to each season, inviting them to stop in and see you when they are in town. You've built a new customer!

Many tourists turn into full-time residents after a pleasant experience when visiting a community. Form a relationship with your Welcome Wagon group or any other type of organization that deals in welcoming newcomers to your community. Surveys show people tend to continue to shop with the first store where they are genuinely welcomed. Put your name on the top of every new resident's shopping list by advertising in New Shopper Guides. Place your advertising materials with real estate offices and utility offices where new residents go to have their services turned on.

Offer a first-timers discount or a welcome reward to new customers; it could be a 10% discount of a small gift item. Advertise in church bulletins and school newspapers if these ads are accepted. Churches and schools are the first places new residents will visit. Show your support of these community activities and your business will be noticed by newcomers to town.

Now Give Me a "T" . . . What does that spell?
Yes - $$$$$

In my first book, *"What Mother Never Told Ya About Retail"* I talked about the t-shirts I used as giveaways during back-to-school and special activities. In my second book, *"52 Promotions"*, I reiterated the point several times, discussing many stores who used t-shirts as g-w-p's to increase their sales and visibility. If - no, I mean - when, I finish this book, I'll say the same thing over again until you finally listen:

T-shirts are one of the very best advertising tools available to apparel store owners. They can be used in combination promotions - either given away or sold at a reduced price, and customers will wear them forever. I once read, and have passed this information on many times, that the average printed message t-shirt has a life span of seven years. The latest research announced by the Jerzees Activewear firm proved me right.

Their findings show that 93% of all adults own at least one printed message t-shirt and that over 15% have had their oldest at least a decade. I pondered this for a few minutes, went to my own closet, and found a shirt from 1971. Unless I discover another one when we pack to move, that is my oldest, which means it's 28 years old!

Customers appreciate the gift and will wear your t-shirts all around town as a walking advertisement. Wouldn't that give you terrific image exposure? Create an attractive pleasing graphic design - possibly humorous, that women would be proud to wear. Then give them away! It works! You have the ideal item for church auctions, for school door prizes, for that little extra "thank you" to the special customer who brought in three relatives to shop. Some stores even sell these, marking them as high as $20 to make the perceived value of the shirt higher.

The survey said people kept t-shirts the longest that they received from the following:

Charity Events	24%
Other	23%*
Company/Product	15%*
School Event	9%
Concert	7%
Bought for self	6%
Trip	6%
Gift	2%

* If you still are doubtful about having t-shirts made for your business, just order a few. A local screen printer will do a minimum order as low as 18 or so, as long as you paid for the screen. Give them to your employees, family and close friends and watch the reaction. I promise you'll re-order in a few days. (You probably want to order all large and extra large, even petites like their t-shirts to fit large and many will use them for swimsuit coverups and nightshirts.)

Hitting You Advertising Target
By Rick Segel

The question is how and why do customers come to the store? Do you know? Have you ever stopped to figure out why? Is it because of your windows? Is it due to referrals or happy customers? Are your newspaper ads so strong that they pull them in? Maybe it's your radio or TV spots. It could be because of a certain line you carry or even because of a favorite salesperson. Whatever the reasons are, find out what is bringing the customers in your store.

The more I consult with businesses, the more amazed I get that they don't know where their business is coming from. The scary part is that they *think they know* where their business is coming from. They might be right, BUT the fear is that they might be wrong. I have seen businesses continue to run ads in the local papers, not because they worked, but just because they have always done it . You want to spend your promotional dollars in areas that have the greatest return.

How do you do it? *You simply ASK!* Even ask your old steady customers why they like to shop with you. Create a list of reasons why customers come in or buy at the store. Just check off every customer by reason. You might be surprised. Don't worry about any embarrassment from the customers - they will appreciate it and will gain respect for you as a business person. Once you know, you can target your advertising at the bull's eye!

The Science of Wowing
by Rick Segel

What is it? A **WOW** is a brief moment of amazement. It occurs when you see something different or something you don't expect to see. It astounds and impresses people. A **WOW** is a positive reaction to an event. When you exceed someone's expectations, it becomes a **WOW.**

I had fallen in love with the concept of **WOW**ing 25 years ago when I was thrown into the retail business without any experience. My father became sick and I was there to help out. I observed an amazing phenomenon. When a customer came into the store, saw something and said, **"WOW,"** I knew a sale was imminent. The normal speech pattern was **"WOW'**, then quickly followed with a *"that's different,"* then *"I'll take it."*

My goal then became to work toward creating **WOW**'s, since they would eventually turn into sales. A good analogy might be when someone teaches you how to howl. Get the ball to roll over those marks and forget about the pins. Focus on the WOWs and the sale will just naturally follow. It becomes a philosophy, a way to structure your business and life. It becomes a management strategy and part of your business mission.

The aspect I like the most about **WOW**ing is the subconscious thought process it produces to help focus your efforts. It can't be a **WOW** if you are not constantly raising the bar. Second, it focuses toward being different and different sells. Third, it avoids the disease of metooisms (me too isms), It's the leaders who get the glory - not the one who try to jump on the band wagon later. **WOW**ing avoid that because you are striving for the best.

WOWing is a way to conduct your business life. I believe it is an acronym that stands for a *"Wonderful Opportunity to Win"* - to win customers and make them true believers. Make sure you are dedicated to finding the best **WOW**s so you can **WOW** your customers!

Hiring The Right Employee

With the current shortage of workers, I realize it is tempting to hire the first person who actually fills out an application, but STOP. Don't jump into something without conducting an interview and finding out if this is the right person for your job opening.

Judy Billings of Seattle gave me this interview question advice many years ago, and it is as valuable today as it was then. Judy said by using this system she found her employees staying for three years, rather than three months. Think of the training costs she saved, not to mention the additional sales, because all of her staff was knowledgeable and product savvy.

Key Points of Interviewing:

(1) Make the candidate comfortable. Offer a beverage. Chit chat a bit before you stat asking questions. Each interview could take up to 45 minutes (no longer), but no less than 20 minutes.

(2) Ask the person if it's ok for you to take notes. (It's important that you follow the exact procedure for every candidate. By taking notes you'll listen and understand better,)

(3) Have a written job description of what is expected and what they will receive in return. Ask direct questions and expect direct, complete answers.

Job Description: Sales Person - Average $75 per hour in sales required

Sample questions:

Do you have any problems working peek hours, weekends or overtime?

Who are your favorite customers? Your least favorite customer types?

What is the largest sale you ever made? How do you do it? Do you maintain a customer book?

Why do you think you would make a great sales person here in his store?

What is the classic skirt length? What are the rules for selecting earrings for a face shape?

Job Description: Merchandising and Display

Sample questions:

What merchandising technique do you think help sell garments?

What's the best display you ever made? Where? How much was the overall cost?

What is personal favorite place to shop?

Job Description: Organizational skills- bookkeeping - receptionist

Sample questions:

The phone is ringing, you have a customer in front of the mirror. Another just walked in, and someone is at the counter to pay. How would you handle this situation? What type of paper work duties have you done in the past? Do you know how to operate a computer? Do you like desk jobs? Will you work the sales floor if needed in an emergency situation?

The list can go on and on, but until you decide what to ask the prospective employee, you won't get the answers you need. Interviews can determine the personality and capability of a future employee. Take time to do it right the first time to avoid the same scenario next week.

After hiring your employee, give them your employee handbook (a sample is on the following pages) and have them sign your employment agreement showing they have read the handbook and are in agreement to the terms of your employee contract.

Give the Kids A Chance - Hire Student Workers

When I was very young I went to work at a local department store. To this day, I thank that man for giving me an opportunity to pursuit my dream of a life in fashion. am today because . Isn't there some young person out there somewhere who could be feeling that way about you?

When looking for new employees, when needing more help, this is the time to think about part-time student workers. Is the work load too much for your present staff, but perhaps not quite enough to justify another full-time employee?

The solution to your labor problem is right there in your own neighborhood. Look to the local community college, university or even high school. Students need experience - you need help. Most are wiling to work for minimum wages and will work flexible hours. As a trainee, students are glad to get the work, some of which may even be used to apply as class projects for credit in certain related courses.

The major enticement for college students is the EXPERIENCE. They are in need of good letters of reference and notations that will look good on their resumes. The opportunity to actively participate in a real-job environment while still in school gives them samples of their work and records of their work ethic to show prospective employers down the line after graduation.

High school students are usually looking for extra money (to spend on clothing) and the status of working in what they consider a glamourous job in fashion. The employee discount is also very appealing. These employees make great walking advertisements.

Finding these students is easier than you think. Notify the school guidance counselor, post your notices on the student union bulletin board, advertise in the school paper, or contact a club or group on campus.

If you approach the dean, department head, or instructor in appropriate departments, your information will reach a select group interested in fashion merchandising, marketing, or advertising work. Many of these officials are willing to take on projects as part of the class course. i.e. I know stores who have college classes complete demographic surveys, design advertising plans, create store logos and do in-store and window displays as part of class credit.
Students compete against each other or work together as teams and are graded on the final results at the end of the semester.

Payment for this type of work is based on a variety of factors, including the pay scale in your area, the degree of difficulty of the project and the expenses the students have incurred. You can sit down with the individual student or the professor , if this is a group project, and determine how much time the job will take. (If it is to decorate the two large windows twice a month, you calculate the in store work time, plus allot time for the design and creativity and materials not supplied by store.) You may want to say, *"Is $25 enough for this?"* If not, then deal up. Remember, you can never deal down.

<u>Final tips for enticing students to work for you:</u>
(1) Always mention in your ad *"This will look great on your resume."*
(2) Remember these are students. If they were skilled pros, they wouldn't still be in school.
(3) Be willing to serve as a mentor. Share your skills and expertise.
(4) Be selective. There are lots of young people out there. Choose well.
(5) Check with your accountant to be sure you comply with all employment tax and labor laws. In some cases you may qualify for matching government funds for student payroll assistance.

Educate The TEAM!

Remember the old adage: *You can have the most wonderful merchandise in the world, but if it doesn't sell - you still got it!* You may be a terrific buyer, a talented display artist, an advertising guru, but....you can not do it all and finally your fate ends up in the hands of a sales associate. Foolishly many of us tend to hire someone, give them five minutes of advice and push them out on the sales floor.

SPRING TRAINING: There is a definite reason that baseball players spend several weeks preparing for the regular season - everyone is out of practice. Don't you think your staff feels the same let down after the Christmas rush and the January Sale excitement has faded? Like any skill, customer service and sales training needs a workout. I don't guess we could act like baseball managers and "cut" people from the squad if they didn't pass training, but you know - we should. Don't allow a long time employee to get in their own rut of doing it their way - every day. This is YOUR store. You make the rules and they supposedly follow them.

Pre-season training can improve sales when cash-flow is at a normal low and also encourage and ready employees for the traffic that will be picking up at the first ray of sunshine and melting snow. Why not have *"Spring Training"* incentives for your staff? (Read some of Bob Nelson's suggestions in 101 Ways to Reward Your Employees or Ed Falk's 1001 Ways to Create Retail Excitement: both books are excellent sources of inspiration when dealing with staff rewards.

Isn't 16 years of school enough? There is no limit to learning, but you'll find it is sometimes very difficult to teach old fashion mavens new tricks. In other words - YOU! Successful business people should consider themselves "lifetime learners." That is the reason you should take every available opportunity to attend seminars at market and industry events such as my semi-annual Retail Retreat. This is a renewal for your mind and body. Learning new and different things, as well as reviving old *good* habits long forgotten will revitalize you and your bottom line.(After every seminar someone will say, *"We used to do that and it was great?"* I always want to say, *"Why did Ya stop?"* but I know the answer. Things just get tiring, boring and common, and we burn-out.

A successful store owner is never satisfied with even the most successful techniques of here and now. They should always be looking forward to the horizon and what's ahead. Before you can train your staff, you yourself should feel energized and you must be able to understand a few basic facts about adult learning.

"Why do I have to color *inside* the line?" Unlike children who are more apt to follow instructions and respect authority, adults need to know WHY they need to know. When it comes to training, you must clearly convey the relevancy of everything that is taught. Before trying to teach, be sure you can justify the practical application of each point to yourself. If not, leave it out because they won't listen or understand either. Is what you are saying of any importance to the performance of the employee? Will it benefit the store or the staff in a profitable way or is it just a pet peeve of yours? Be firm, be confident, be aggressive.

Understand also that teaching someone to do something doesn't mean the new education will automatically be put to use. That is probably the most frustrating part of presenting seminars and classes. The training's effectiveness is ultimately up to the sales associate, but there are ways to improve your chances of it being put to use out on the sales floor. Remember, adults like to be involved in the solution - not just told what works and what doesn't. Let them take part by asking questions that require their participation. Ask them to come up with different sales situations that may create problems. Be sure to call on each employee during every training session.

The more senses experienced in the learning process, the more permanent the comprehension. Most adults will remember over 90% of what they *say and do*, so don't just rattle off lists of guidelines. If there is a list, print it and give each person a copy. Post it on a staff bulletin board. Give them things to take home and read. Have each and every person take part in acting out selling scenes on the sales floor. Adults learn by DOING - not by being *told or shown*.

Reward Employees? How? When? How Much?
The Pros and Cons of Direct Types of Rewards

When the holiday season rolled around in 1998 for Ty Warner, President and sole owner of Ty, Inc., probably better known to the world as the Beanie Baby Company, he made an amazing decision. For a Christmas bonus, each employee - from the janitor, all the way up to the national manager, received one years salary. This is in addition to the special employee-only edition Beanies they receive on a regular basis. Wow, can you imagine such a reward?

Perhaps this wasn't what he had in mind, but here are some other choices that you may find beneficial. Rewarding employees with the wrong type of reward or message can do more damage than no reward at all. Pay close attention to these pros and cons when making your decisions:

MONEY
Con: Once the employee spends the money, the reward is quickly forgotten; also if you use cash rewards often, employees tend to lump them in with their base salary, diminishing the value as a motivational tool.
Pro: It's value is self-evident; anyone can use it, and recipients can decide what to do with it.

MERCHANDISE
Con: You need to decide on merchandise far in advance and make sure it's available when the time comes; it can be difficult to guess what employees will value or work toward.
Pro: Has *"brag value"* to the employee, who can show off his or her prize to friends and family.

PLAQUES/TROPHIES
Con: Plaques and trophies have little practical value, which may limit their usefulness as rewards.
Pro: Some people really like to win a *prize!* These can be customized for employees; they honor specific behavior, and they will last a lifetime. Again there is the brag factor.

Recognize and Reward Employees

According to author and management consultant Rosabeth Moss Kanter, "*Recognition - saying thank you in public and perhaps giving a tangible gift along with the words - has multiple functions beyond simple human courtesy. To the employee, recognition signifies that someone noticed and someone cares. What is the point of going all out to do something special if no one notices and it does not seem to make a difference? To the rest of the organization, recognition creates role models - heroes - and communicates the standards. These are the kinds of things that constitute great performance around here.*"

<u>Here are some guidelines for successfully recognizing employees</u>:

(1) Emphasize success rather than failure. You tend to miss the positive if you are busily searching for the negatives.

(2) Deliver recognition and reward in an open and publicized way. If not made public recognition loses much of its impact and defeats much of the purpose for which it is provided.

(3) Deliver recognition in a personal and honest manner. Avoid providing recognition that is too "slick" or overproduced.

(4) Tailor your recognition and reward to the unique needs of the people involved. Having many recognition and reward options will enable management to acknowledge accomplishment in ways appropriate to the particulars of a given situation, selected from a larger menu of possibilities.

(5) Timing is crucial. Recognize contribution throughout a project. Reward contributions close to the time an achievement is realized. Time delays weaken the impact of most rewards.

(6) Strive for a clear, unambiguous and well-communicated connection between accomplishments and rewards. Be sure people understand why they receive awards and the criteria used to determine rewards.

(7) Recognize recognition. That is, recognize people who recognize others for doing what is best for the company.

"*It's up to you to decide how to speak to your people. Do you single out individuals for public praise and recognition? Make people who work for you feel important. If you honor and serve them, they'll honor and serve you.*"....MARY KAY ASH

It's Time For Sales Training In-Store

"It's what you learn after you know it all that really counts!" No truer words have ever been spoken, especially regarding ladies apparel retailers and their sales staff.

Yet one of the most difficult chores in operating a store is training the staff. Why? Because they know it all. The new ones think it's easy; the veterans think they've seen it all, and neither group wants to spend any time to learn to do a better job. No one ever thinks they need what they really need, so it's up to you to turn them into sales associates, rather than space holders on the sales floor. Are you qualified for *this* job?

The secret to making the most of the least amount of training time lies in your ability to maximize and respect that time. Plan ahead - be ready and make it interesting and informative.

Make a list of the issues you'd like to discuss. People are more likely to tune in if they know you've taken time to organize a session. Truly good sales trainers are few and far between so if you're not one - hire somebody or have your top sales leader offer their suggestions. (Be careful of job envy. Some may turn a deaf ear just because she is the top sales leader!).

The trainer should outline their thoughts on paper at least one day prior to the training meeting. Post this outline to let everyone know what they are covering in the grand scheme of things. Keep your session limited to the agenda posted for that day. If it's greeting the customer, co-ordination of outfits, accessorizing or friendly role playing, stay on that topic for this session. Don't swing over to layaways or why the trash can wasn't emptied last night.

When the group gets together it is very easy to lose control and have the entire session turn into a social atmosphere with conversations about everything except sales training. Don't let this happen. Plan store meetings, parties or other activities for that. Remember **sales training is education**. Be the teacher, help your staff learn - so they will sell more and you'll profit!

What a Great Employee IDEA!

Building a team is easier if your people all know each other on a personal level. Sometimes this is impossible because the part-timers all work different schedules or the seamstresses and bookkeeping people work in a different part of the store. Friendship and camaraderie don't happen by themselves. You can help by throwing an after-hours staff party where employees can socialize and get to know each other.

Create a *staff yearbook* form. Ask personal questions about their favorite music, the last movie they saw, their dream job, names of their pets or children, their ideal weekend, etc. While the staff mingles, have each fill out their form. Take Polaroids and attach them to the completed questionnaires. Hang the *yearbook* information in the break room for everyone to enjoy. Later, compile the forms and the photos into a yearbook binder. As you hire new people, show them the yearbook to help them get acquainted with their co-workers - and have them add their own questionnaire during their training.

The 10 Biggest Mistakes Sales Associates Make

(1) Knowing everything about everything!
(2) Thinking the customer is stupid.
(3) Prejudging the customer's buying power.
(4) Disregarding the customer's needs.
(5) Not knowing when to shut up and listen.
(6) Lack of product knowledge,
(7) Not recognizing "I want to buy" signals.
(8) Being overly aggressive when selling.
(9) Not being warm and friendly.
(10) Not presenting yourself as a professional.

Listen to the customer - Learn what they need - Make the SALE!

Yes, I know many customers just drop by to visit, to have that afternoon chat before heading home to start dinner or spend another boring evening in front of the television, but...are you listening when they talk? It could mean $$$$$.

This is how we learn to use selling opportunities that are often overlooked. Active listening requires not only full attention to the customer's comments, but also: nodding, leaning forward, and maintaining eye contact. Add a short verbal acknowledgment such as, *"I see,"* or *"Yes, I know how that is."* Pay attention to details. Did she mention trip? Then quickly say, *"You'll be needing a new outfit for your sister's wedding."* Or maybe she's been exercising, *"If you've been walking, I bet you've lost inches, let's try on a new size and see if the hard work is paying off."*

Where's the Problem?

According to the White House Office of Consumer Affairs:

- An average business will never hear from 96% of its customers who are unhappy with some aspect of the service they received.

- For every complaint a business receives 26 other customers have a problem that they never report. Six of these problems are considered really serious in the minds of the customers.

- Those customers who don't complain to the business will complain ABOUT the business to up to 10 people.

- Complainers are more likely than non-complainers to do business with a company again, ever if the complaint is not resolved to their satisfaction.

- Customers whose complaints are effectively resolved tell an average of five other people.

Sales Safari - A Hunting Season for Your Staff

What is The Sales Safari?

Based on the key elements of a full-day seminar entitled RUN WITH THE LIONS selling skills workshop, the **Sales Safari** is a self-paced, skill development program designed specifically for retail sales associates and frontline managers. The concept (developed with the input of hundreds of sales associates, store field managers and retail trainers) produces outstanding results because it takes associates and their coaches through the following four levels of learning. . .

Level One: Reaction - The **Sales Safari** is designed with retail associates in mind. The program is short, to the point, focused on the 20% of the sales activities that produce 80% of the sales results for the majority of people. And it's fun!

Level Two: Understanding - Using what the authors, Andrea & Richard refer to as the *"Selling Styles Matrix"*, this program introduces participants to four specific selling styles, contrasting the differences and providing a clear picture of what a sales lion is. Understanding the attitudes *(thoughts)* and actions *(behaviors)* of these styles provide learners with a framework for asking themselves in a given sales situation, *"What would a Lion do?"*

Level Three: Use - The **Sales Safari** isn't just another book participants read and then forget. Each activity-based "expedition" helps associates and managers develop high-impact selling skills quickly... in small-bites...and allowing them to put these skills to use immediately.

Level Four: Results! - Participants go at their own pace. Then once they feel comfortable they see the manager/trainer who will test their ability to demonstrate mastery and have their workbook dated and stamped to verify completion of that expedition. The entire program can usually be completed during low customer traffic periods right on the sales floor, often in 30 days or less.

The **Sales Safari** is unique because it actually acts as two development tools in one. Not only do sales associates improve their selling skills, but the program simultaneously improves the coaching and development skills of your frontline manager or yourself.

How Expeditions are Organized . . . Each has six specific parts to it:

(1) Surveying the Landscape previews the specific skill and explains why it is important.

(2) Safari Snapshots gives a brief overview of how the various selling styles behave.

(3) Following in a Lion's Footsteps shows the participant what to do and how to do it,

(4) Reviewing The Critical Steps provides an at-a-glance recap of the steps covered.

(5) Sharpening Your Skills provides specific exercises to help associates develop the skill.

(6) Journey's End is where the associate gets her chance to demonstrate mastery of the skill!

THE **SALES SAFARI** is a workbook, trainer's guide and video. In today's world where good help is hard to find, and even harder to train and retain, I wholeheartedly recommend this training course for your employees. Call for Richard or Andrea today at **1-800-290-5028.** It's a jungle out there. Isn't it time you bagged the business? This is your license to hunt - don't let shopping season pass you by.

Overcoming Customers Procrastination

Assuming that you have presented all the facts that are necessary for a customer to make a buying decision, one reason may remain for procrastination: *The buyer is afraid of making the wrong decision.* She would rather take the easy way out and do nothing at all than make a purchase she will not be happy with later.

Did you ever notice how fast professionals will react when they're in their own area of expertise? Like you, at market, when you say, *"This one, that one - not that one - four of this - all red - no pink."* For a more drastic example - a surgeon makes a split-second decision on the operating table because the smallest hesitation could cause death.

Then once removed from these familiar surroundings where they are trained to act with precision, sometimes these same people are unable to make what appears to be, in comparison, a very minor decision. *"Which color shirt should I get?"*

The result is people not wanting to risk making the wrong choice today = delay! On the other hand, shoppers will rarely procrastinate when they know that buying is absolutely the right thing to do and their choice is a good one.

YOU must present the case for your merchandise so convincingly that your customer is comfortable trusting your recommendation. How does that happen?

☻ Show her the need for the item.

☻Explain how she can use it to build her wardrobe choices or add to an outfit.

☻Tell her how attractive it is, and how it compliments her face or body shape.

☻ Explain the easy-care instructions and compare the price and value.

☻ Have a reputation that she trusts.

Here are two common objections and an answer to use to overcome each:

"Well, I like it but I will think about it and let you know."...Speak with confidence in your voice and say, *"Now Joyce, this is just perfect for you, and we have already seen how wonderful it matches your suit from last season. Go ahead and take it home on approval and see how you like it with your accessories."*. . . It probably will not be returned.

"It's too early to buy now. I'll get it when I start planning my winter trip.". . . You quickly reply... *"Yes, but there are only two of these in your size and I would hate for them to all be gone when you come back next month. Why not take it today when we can have time to alter it, steam it, and have it ready for you to pack for your trip on time? That'll be one less last minute thing to worry about then."*

I can not stress how important it is to role play this type of situation over and over again with your staff in sales meetings or just on a slow Wednesday afternoon. If no customers are around, instruct your staff to *"sell"* to each other.

One of my favorite people is Libby Cockerham of Jon Marc Department Store in West Jefferson, North Carolina. I can always count on Libby to fill me in on the latest happenings at retail and I enjoy comparing employee data and business information with her. She is always willing to share her experience and expertise with other store owners.

When Libby feels like employees are at lost for something to do when times are slow in the store, she hands them her *"Libby List - Fifty Nifty Things to Do When You Don't Have A Customer."* This is a great idea. I suggest you copy it to fit your individual needs, then laminate and keep it on hand for that slow Thursday afternoon when your crew is just standing around.

It would be wonderful if everyone was a self-starter who would automatically pick up the phone and start calling customers or addressing birthday cards or sending thank you notes, but it's not going to work that way. I think you had better prepare your list.

Fifty Nifty Things to Do
When You Don't Have A Customer

1. Empty Hanger Box
2. Vacuum dressing rooms.
3. Dust shelves in dressing rooms.
4. Dust pantry shelves.
5. Dust jewelry cases.
6. Check for & clean tarnished jewelry
7. Clean mirrors, doors, glass tables
8. Size merchandise on t-racks & walls
9. Create outfits & accessories them
10. Change displays on the walls
11. Run shoe box inventory
12. Dust shoe boxes & shelves
13. Dust t-rack bottoms
14. Straighten underneath the counters
15. Check layaway
16. Fill pin cushions
17. Dust handbags
18. Clean bathrooms
19. Wash dishes in employee room
20. Restock plastic hangers in box
21. Call customers in profile book
22. Check back stock items
23. Restock hosiery bin
24. Check lingerie stock with book
25. Check dresses for sizes, buttons, belts
26. Start a video in VCR
27. Change wicker busts
28. Straighten drawers and label them
29. Clean around wrapping counter
30. Vacuum steps
31. Clean glass cubes for mens shirts
32. Go through the hold tickets
33. Carry hangers to stock room
34. Spot mop areas that need
35. Straighten sizers by size
36. Organize sale signs
37. Clean sewing room
38. Clean out refrigerator
39. Dust banister & railing to basement
40. Wash makeup mask & footies
41. Dust louver doors
42. Clean trophies& plaques
43. Sweep sidewalk & entrance
44. Restock ribbons & tape
45. Restock paper bags
46. Reticket returns and return to stock
47. Steam odds & ends and pick into stock
48. Straighten hangers ins stockroom
49. Get cobwebs off the awnings
50. Refer to the beginning of this list. By now, it's time to start over again!

Employee Theft - Yes, It Happens to All of Us

One out of every five employees steal from their employers. Unbelievable? Yes, I know I can hear you gasping, "Not in my store." But it's happening and though most small store owners are in a state of denial, it is costing billions of dollars each year in lost income.

A recent survey by Reid Psychological Systems of Chicago points out that over the course of the three year study, part-timers who admitted to cash thefts, stole 33% more than full-time employees. This poll was drawn from data taken in a nationals survey of more than 15,000 workers in retailer businesses all across the U.S.

The average cash theft admitted by part-time employees was $414.61, compared to $311.18 for a full-time employee. The study also indicated that a part-time employee takes 47% more merchandise than their full-time co-workers.

It is almost impossible to stop a determined thef, but it is easy to discourage the temptation. Don't make it so easy! Pay attention to details.

Here are some tips to follow:

Use numbered sales tickets. If a ticket is missing, FIND it. Make all employees accountable by requiring voids be approved by managers. All voided sales tickets should be kept and filed.

Watch for the switch. Thieves learn how to skim by ringing up a small sale, collecting a larger amount and pocketing the difference, or by destroying the entire sales ticket. Audit the cash drawer frequently and sometimes unannounced. Be on the lookout for unauthorized discounts or returns. An employee may be ringing up a $99 item as a $9 item and receiving a kickback later from their accomplice.

Check the trash. Many items are sneaked out in the daily trash bags. Check them randomly and make sure all boxes leaving the stock room are actually empty. Check all boxes that have been packed for postal or UPS delivery. Were these actually purchases or just merchandise being sent to an accomplice outside the store.

Don't make it so easy. The person who checks in the deliveries and the person who checks in inventory should not be the same person. You need a backup plan to secure merchandise makes it to the sales floor.

Hire a spy. Remember only the employees who steal have anything to worry about. Find an outside person to come in and review your internal operations.

Be obvious. Store owners can prevent over 50% of internal theft by just announcing that they are watching for it! Be open about it; explain you are on the lookout for loss, and encourage all employees to help.

Be serious. If you discover employee theft, do not cover it up or ignore it. Fire the person and seriously consider filing suit. This is a CRIME - treat it as such.

Stay on top of your business and be the person in charge. The employee who claims to *"treat it as if it were her* own *business"* may actually be doing just that, and taking home the profits at the end of the day, too. **BEWARE!**

You're the Person in Charge - A/K/A THE BOSS

You fulfilled your dream. You are now the owner of your own store selling gifts or fashion apparel. Life is going to be just wonderful . . . or is it? Suddenly you discover that in addition to buying, selling, displaying, bookkeeping, housekeeping, advertising, etc. you are now also somebody's BOSS. Thank goodness, that means there will be somebody there to help with all those other jobs I just listed. Right? Yes, but only if you do your job correctly.

These people are working for you for a reason - the main one being most people do not have the desire, the determination and/or the resources to own their own businesses. Therefore they seek jobs in the public workplace, and now are depending on you. A survey by the labor department shows that of all people:

> 75% need a boss
> 23% need supervision
> 2% are self-starters *

You are in the 2%* but don't expect to find any of those types applying at your store. Your employees will need direction, supervision, a chain of command, and a company policy.

The following pages contain an excellent company policy handbook sample. Add your name and print for your business. Add or delete items, change the wordings, but use this as a basis for your handbook today. Don't wait until problems occur, you need this now.

The first page is an agreement statement that the employee has read the handbook and agrees to adhere to your policies and company rules. Put the signed copy in your files and give the employee one to keep.

MY STORE
1234 Main Street
Anywhere, USA 00045
506-777-5432

My Store Employee Handbook Verification Statement

INTRODUCTION:

There are rules of conduct that are necessary to any well managed operation for the benefit and well being of all. This handbook serves as a guideline for employees in order that there is a clear understanding of what is expected of every employee.

Achieving our goals together in harmony with respect, team effort and determination is our task. If all are committed to cooperation, then flexibility will be possible. A positive attitude, honesty and professionalism are required at all times. These are the basic ingredients of success in a business.

Employees are expected to read this policy handbook, digest all the guidelines for store behaviors, and then proceed to use their own best judgement in situations. Repeated disregard for these policies may result in:
(1) Verbal and written reprimand
(2) Warning
(3) Discharge when warranted

By observing these guidelines, you can insure a businesslike, efficient, and pleasant working situation for everyone involved from owners to management to employees. This handbook is not intended to imply any contract or contractual rights.

Please sign and date below to acknowledge that you have received and understand fully this employee handbook. This letter will be kept in your employee file with your job application and W-2 tax information.

_____   _____
Employee Name   Social Security #

Dated:_____

My Store
1234 Main Street
Anywhere, USA 00045
506-777-0543

Hours of Operation

Store hours are: 10:00 A.M. - 5:30 P.M. - Monday-Friday
10:00 A.M. - 5:00 P.M. - Saturday
Occasional Special Event Openings on Sunday

Since the store officially opens at 10:00, morning shifts should clock in no later than 9:45 A.M. in order to have enough time to prepare the store for opening. On occasion, late customers may delay the normal closing time, and you may be asked to stay late if possible to accommodate these shoppers.

Payday

Paydays are bi-monthly, every other Friday. Under no circumstances will paychecks be issued early or in advance of actually work provided. A discharged employee will be paid in full no later than the sixth day after discharge, and other employees who leave will be paid no later than the next scheduled payday.

Overtime

Your normal work scheduled is devised in order to eliminate overtime or at least keep it to a minimum. Overtime may result from closing delays due to late customers, or because of my schedule or special events for which I may ask an employee to work additional hours. Productive overtime is very acceptable. Please note, overtime accumulates (40 hours per week); therefore, if an employee alters the work schedule for personal reasons during one week of the pay period, the *lost time* cannot be made up the next week of the two-week pay period if it would result in the week of the pay period exceeding 40 hours. Overtime hours are compensated by. time-and-one-half wages.

Lunch Break

Each employee is allowed one hour for lunch break. Sometimes, due to customer demands, lunch hours are not predictable, but you are still entitled to a one-hour break. You may remain in the store and use our kitchen room if you desire, but please take advantage of your one-hour time as it cannot be counted as an additional work hour day. During peak retail periods, as per my instructions, a shorter lunch period may be permissible for which the extra time will be paid if applicable.

Definition of Employee

Full-time employees: Normal weekly schedule of 40 hours or more
Part-time employees: Normal weekly schedule of 39 hours or less.

Sick Days or Paid Leave

Full-time employees are entitled to 7 paid sick/personal days a year (January 1st - December 31st). Payment is based on a seven (7) hour work day. Non-paid optional days off may be taken as long as a replacement has been secured and permission granted. This should not become excessive and conflict with our regular schedule. Unused sick days can not be carried over to the next calendar year.

Vacation Time

Full-time employees are eligible for vacation with pay in accordance with the following schedule:

Employed:
6 months - 2 years: 1 week paid vacation (based on 40 hours per week, Jan.1 - Dec. 31)
2 years or more :   2 weeks paid vacation (Jan. 1 - Dec. 31)

When scheduling vacations, please give ample notice. Please try not to schedule vacation time from November 18th through January 15th as this is a very busy time in our retail business. Employees will not be compensated for unused vacation or sick/personal days upon dismissal or quitting. One week only of unused vacation may be carried over to the next year (if permission is asked in advance).

Paid Holidays

The following five holidays are paid based on a 7 hour day:

New Year's Day
July 4th
Thanksgiving Day
Christmas Day
Your Birthday*

*Should you decide to work on your birthday, you will receive your days work pay, as well as your birthday days pay, but this will not be included in your hourly schedule resulting in overtime.

Absenteeism and Tardiness

Everyone occasionally runs late. If you know you are going to be late, please call _____ at _____ or the manager. Being tardy or absent without good reason more than 6 times a year is considered excessive and is a violation of company attendance standards.

> 4 absences or tardies - a written warning will be issued
> 6 absences or tardies - probation
> 7 absences or tardies are grounds for dismissal

A no-show or a no-call to _____ without legitimate reason may result in dismissal.

Employee Discounts

Employees of MY SPECIALTY SHOP are entitled to a 30% discount on all regular priced merchandise sold in the store, excluding any consignment or special trunk show items. (A discount for these will be determined on an individual item basis by _____.) Additional discounts will be used as sales incentives or rewards during certain periods. You may use your employee discount for purchases for yourself and your *immediate family only* (your spouse, or unmarried children living within your home). *You may also purchase gifts, but not excessively.* If you are found to be abusing this agreement, this practice will result in immediate dismissal. Please give the customers first-choice on items; re-orders can be made to fulfill your needs.

Employee Charges & Layaways

Employee charge accounts should never at any time exceed your $500 credit limit. You will not be allowed to special order or purchase anything until this balance is paid down. We are happy to allow you to place special orders at your 30% discount but on special orders, you must pay in full in advance rather than using your charge account. When special orders are placed - please consider this purchased. Do not rely on selling it as it would increase my inventory which is carefully planned at market.

Regular mercandise taken on approval will be charged to your account after 3 days. If this results in your credt limit being exceeded, then you will need to pay cash for the merchandise no later than the 4th day. Layaway rules apply to employees the same as regular customers. Employees are NOT allowed to hold items in the back for their preference. Everything should either be charged, paid, or written up on approval - do not tag items with your name and expect them to remain out of our of inventory.

Employees tickets are to be either written by _____ or another authorized employee. At no time should you write your own charge ticket or payment on account. You are also no allowed to cash personal checks or otherwise take money from the cash drawer at any time. If this is necessary, ask _____ for assistance and authorization.

Store Keys

Store keys are distributed to certain key employees. Do not loan or give this key to anyone or allow any person to use it without your presence. Do not go to the store during non-business hours without prior permission from _____. Always lock the store behind you when in the store during non-business hours and admit no one without authorization. The keys are the property of _____and in the event you are no longer an employee of My Specialty Store, the keys must be returned to _____at once.

Drugs

My Specialty Store has a duty to provide a safe work environment. The company prohibits the use, possession, sales or transfer of illegal drugs on or off company property. My Specialty Shop prohibits use, possession or being under the influence of alcohol or drugs on company property or while conducting business. Employees taking any medication that can cause any degree of impairment should tell _____ or the manager.

Grievances or Complaints

Any complaint should be reported to the manager. If necessary, you may bypass the manager and communicate the problem directly to _____. It is store policy to maintain confidentiality of any and all complaints.

Smoking Policy

My Specialty Store is a non-smoking building. Anyone caught smoking within the confines of the building, restrooms, stock rooms, etc. could face possible immediate dismissal. The front door area and immediate parking lot are also off-limits to employee smoking.   You may smoke behind the store (outside the back entrance) , during your morning or afternoon break, but keep this area clean of cigarette butts and debris. It is suggested that you use mouth wash or breath spray before returning to the sales floor if you have been smoking.

Dress Code

All employees of My Specialty Store are expected to represent the store and dress accordingly. Casual dressing does not belong in a better women's specialty store, however, we will offer "casual Fridays" or "special days" which means if you choose, you may wear black or denim (no faded or with holes) jeans with a blazer, sweater or fashionable vest. *When in doubt, do not wear it to work*! Tank tops or camisoles should be worn under jackets only in a professional manner. Skirts shorter than your fingertips are not acceptable. Any skirt that is above the knee, including city shorts, should be accessorized with hosiery. Sandals, flip flops and other casual shoes will not be allowed. Again, if in doubt, ask or don't wear. Your wardrobe is an advertisement and a representation of the image of this business. It is as important as your customer service and selling skills, because You are the store. I hope you will take pride in your appearance as a representative of My Specialty Store, not only at work but in your personal life.

Employees Rules of Conduct

(1)   Enthusiasm is contagious - but so is negativism. If you come to work grouchy or depressed, your mood is bound to affect those around you and in turn they are likely to pass it along to each other and the customer, as well.

(2)   Everyone has problems, please leave yours at home.

(3)   Gossiping about your fellow employees is not acceptable, as it is negative and not good for morale. If there is a problem, come to _____ and let us get it out in the open   and finalized. Teamwork is our goal and each person must rely on the assistance and   friendship of each other to achieve our purpose of serving our customers in a friendly and   comfortable atmosphere.

Salary Basis

All employees are paid as agreed in advance of their hiring. Raises will be given on merit and length of employment. The Store does not pay commission wages because we feel this encourages jealousy and over competitiveness in the store among employees. It is our hope that you can work together with customers to provide them with the highest quality fashion consultations available.

Special incentives may be used at times to encourage sales or push certain items. Every employee will have an equal opportunity to enjoy these extra benefits. During your day you may be required to work many areas of the store, including steaming, hanging, unpacking, selling, displaying, gift wrapping, etc.   This is a full-service specialty shop and each employee is expected to carry their load and do what is asked of them. If any of this becomes a problem for you or you feel you are not being given the proper job assignments, mention this to _____. Do not complain to or about each other to other employees.

Store Business and Confidentiality

Do not discuss store business with anyone outside the employ of The Specialty Store. What a customer says or buys in our store is their business and theirs alone. Do not tell your friends or family anything about purchases, finances, or the personal lives of our customers. When a person shops in a store they expect customer service and confidentiality! (Breaking this rule will result in immediate dismissal from our employ.)

Store finances including daily sales amounts, invoice amounts, markups, or any financial information you are aware of is also the strict confidential business of The Specialty Store. If you are allowed access to this information, consider it a trust, and do not break this trust by sharing the information with anyone outside the store. Our pricing policies are standard in the industry and very fair, do not discuss with anyone - this is store business only.

Customer Special Orders

Special orders are a way to increase customer loyalty and satisfaction. They are also a good selling tool. However, it is always a good idea to promote selling what we have in current inventory. A 50% deposit should be obtained on any monogrammed orders. Any other special orders should be authorized by _____ as inventory levels are based on sales and on-order levels. When making special orders, use the pre-printed special order forms and obtain a purchase order # found in the purchased order book. Check with _____ before ordering items for any customer whose account is past due 60 days or more. A deposit is normally required for items special ordered by non-regular customers. This judgement call can be made by _____.

Layaway

One-third down is required to put merchandise on layaway. The merchandise should total at least $25.00. The customer then has 2 months to pay the balance. For example:
  Layaway total $100.00 on September 10
  $33.34 puts in layaway
  $33.33 is due on October 10
  $33.33 final payment is due on November 10

Payments may always be made for more than the required amount, but not less. A $15.00 charge will be incurred if not picked up by the final date. THERE ARE NO RETURNS OR EXCHANGES ALLOWED ON LAYAWAY ITEMS. We are not responsible for the weight gains, weight loss or fashion whims of our customers. Again, there can be a judgement call on exchanges if made by _____ in extreme situations which will not harm or jeopardize the store inventory or policy. Sometimes it is best to restore or gain the customer's loyalty than to argue over a small amount. This is a serious judgement call to be made by _____ or by you if you feel you can properly handle the situation. You are empowered to handle customer service problems when neccessary in _____'s absence. Nothing ventured - nothing gained.

Holds

Merchandise should not be held on the hold rack longer than one week for anyone. Be sure to date it and include a description of the contents and the salesperson's name and number. Items will be returned to the store inventory if not picked up or paid, or charged within the allotted length of time. You should take it upon yourself to notify your customers of this occurrence.

Customer Returns

There is a 7 day return policy in effect on merchandise. If merchandise is returned within 7 days a refund will be given. If it was paid for with a credit card, credit the card account; if it was paid by cash or check, a refund check will be issued. Please never give cash out of the cash drawer for returns. If the merchandise was charged on a store charge account, please credit the store charge. If merchandise is returned past the 7 day limit, store credit only can be issued. Different circumstances arise with different customers regarding the return policy. There are some customers that are not aware of the policy and we must kindly make them aware of it. These are good customers that have never known the policy; however, you will notice that kind and honest customers will seldom abuse the policy. It is a touchy situation on occasion and if you are unsure about handling it, just find_____ to make the contact with them. If I am not in the store, do not allow them to leave the merchandise in the store if at all possible because credit can not be guaranteed without my authorization. The merchandise is theirs until otherwise handled. Again - this is a very rare occurrence and mentioned only as to prepare you for the extremes of this business, should such a problem ever arise.

Shoplifting Notification

If you should become aware of a shoplifter, please notify another employee to assist you. You can not confront a suspected shoplifter until they have left the store.) Laws vary in different areas.) Follow them outside and ask them to remain, but do not put yourself in any danger. Have the other employee contact the police. If the party flees, try to get a description of the person and the vehicle as well as a license #. I repeat, do not ever put yourself in personal danger. The merchandise is not worth any possible injury. If you notice a shopper has an unpaid item in their hand or bag, you may want to ask if it is to be included on the sales ticket or if they are still deciding on the purchase. This will usually handle any "small" problems and avoid embarrassment for everyone involved. Professional shoplifters are much more educated and will find a way to hide items on their person. I repeat - never put yourself in danger to prevent a shoplifter from leaving the premises.

Should there be an unruly customer (excessive verbally abusive, violent, drunken, otherwise appearing out-of-control or dangerous), have an employee call the police. Again do not try to restrain this person; keep yourself safe. Report any unusual occurrences to the manager, such as lewd or abusive language, threatening remarks, threatening or abusive phone calls, exposing private parts, etc. This behavior is not acceptable, and will be properly handled

If at any time you are in the store and feel threatened, notify someone at once. If the party leaves and you are alone, lock the store and remain there until someone can come to assist you. Your safety is of the upmost importance to us at all times.

Restroom Facilities

Our clean and spacious restroom facilities are provided for our customers, as well as our personnel. Your co-operation in keeping these areas spotless will be greatly appreciated. Do not leave personal items out on the counter at any time. There are shelves provided below the sink, but remember - this room is also used by our customers, so do not leave any valuables or medications in this area.

There will be a safe place designated in the store for your handbag and personal items. We are not responsible for these items, but will to the best of our ability, try to maintain the safety and privacy of your possessions , when they are placed in the designated area. Please do not ever go through another employee's belongings, handbags, etc. This is just having common courtesy, honesty, and respect for others.

Kitchen Facilities

We do maintain a refrigerator and microwave for our employees use. Please clean up after yourself. Do not leave spoiled food in the refrigerator or on the counter. Empty the trash can daily and wash all utensils immediately after use. We are not responsible for items left in the kitchen. Do not eat or drink other employee's food without permission.

Parking Areas

There are only a small number of parking spots in the immediate front area of the store. Please do not use these spaces except for unloading items for a few minutes. There is ample parking in the rear of the store, or you may park in the middle of the shopping center parking lot, allowing ample space for customer parking. A safe, lighted environment is provided for you in the parking area. Report any strange or unsual persons you might note hanging around the area. Do not leave personal valuables in clear view in your car; lock your car at all times.

Personal Call Books

You are encouraged to keep personal call book files on customers and use them frequently. There are several ways to record customer information. I will show a variety of methods and you may use the one of your choice which works best for you. I really appreciate any staff member who constantly stays in touch with our customers through the store and through their own personal outside contact. A friend at church, a mother at PTA, a new neighbor - each of these could become a loyal new customer just because of a friendly invitation from you.

Birthday Club

Please make sure each customer is given the opportunity to join our birthday club. Cards are to be kept in order by month and need to be addressed and mailed at least 5 days prior to the dates. Also please keep the used cards for my review, posting the date used, the amount purchased, and the amount of total discount given. A follow-up thank you note should then also be sent.

Thank you cards

Thank you notes are furnished by the store and should be sent on every new customer purchase, no matter how small the amount. On regular customers who haven't been in lately, this is also a nice gesture or if the sale is especially large or for an important event (such as a wedding, class reunion, etc.) Make mention of that in the card, i.e. *"I hope the outfit was perfect for your special day."* The card should be signed by the attending sales associate, followed by the store name.

Extra Shopping/Outside Appointments

The occasion may arise that you can offer outside sales appointments, home shows, or special evening appointments for individuals or groups. If this is of interest to you, please discuss it with _____and we will give it a try. This will be done sparingly and on a probable hour wage plus commission. We are always interested in finding additional ways to make more sales and encourage more area residents to shop with us. Your input on this is genuinely appreciated and will always be noted on your employee file for advancement and raise consideration.

<u>Additional Information You May Want to Include:</u>

_____

_____

_____

_____

_____

P.S. The form on page 89 should be signed by the employee and filed with your W-2 forms and other employee records.

The 12 Most Important Lessons In Specialty Store Retailing

By Bob Nelson

If you are like most specialty store retailers, you're constantly on the lookout for ways to increase your bottom line. And these days, it's a big job that seems to get bigger every day.

Most retailers can be divided into two categories: those who resist change and those who welcome change. Top-selling retailers are in the second category. They not only welcome change, but they also are ready for change and respond to change.

In the battle to generate more sales, the winner isn't always the biggest, but the most resourceful. The secret to greater success is not just having a bunch of theoretical ideas... It is having "Tangible Ideas" you can act upon -- and implementing them more effectively in your business. A proven blueprint for success -- to help take your business in the right direction.

It is clear that specialty store owners must get serious about operating their business, or be prepared to accept stagnant revenues. If you apply the following "12 Details Of Operating Your Retail Business" you'll simplify your efforts, multiply profits, and increase the odds of success. They are based on years of research and the actual experience of dealing with hundreds of small to medium-sized retailers in every region of the country who have achieved an unprecedented high level of success.

1. Know Yourself

Know your interests, skills, abilities, and limitations. Having your own business is more than just creating a job for yourself. To be a successful retailer, there are many personal sacrifices and you have to be willing to make them. Your basic roles are in marketing, finance, administration, and the responsibility of personnel. To get the best results, it is rare for one person to play all these roles equally well. You must know which parts you can handle yourself and which parts you're going to need help with. That's why it's so important to be objective and take a close look at your overall strengths and weaknesses. Ask yourself the following questions:

* Do you know the skills critical to your success?
* Are you adaptable to changing conditions?
* Can you take advice from others?
* Do you always obtain the necessary information to run your business?

2. Plan Ahead

Many stores are run by well-intended people who are not informed about   their own operation. As a specialty store owner, if you don't know the ins and outs of running your business, you'll soon be out of business. According to leading authorities, the main reason 80% of all new businesses fail within the first five years is not money, but the lack of the right information and knowledge. If you want to succeed, the trick is to know how to make right the decisions by implementing an effective business plan. Remember, if you fail to plan, and you might as well plan to fail.

3. Know The Industry

You can gain the greatest competitive edge if you understand the intimate knowledge of doing business. The critical difference is to be able track those obstacles that challenge your future survival:

The Competition - Your competitors size, services, location, marketing approach, type of customers, suppliers, and pricing strategies. The Market Environment - Your local business climate, vacancy rate of commercial space, median household income, level of education, age groups, ethnic population, and the demographics of your potential customers. To thrive and prosper, you must be committed to learn, be clear about your objectives, and have the desire and energy to accomplish your goals.

* Does your area have a population base large enough to support you and the nearby competitors?
* Should you try to appeal to a wider range of customers rather than a small segment of the market?
* Have you seen competitive changes taking place that have affected where customers are shopping?

4. Understand Your Customer

Are you listing to your customers? Make it your business to give your customers what they want, and they will do business and buy from you. They are the reason you are in business, and your future depends on them. The products and services you provide should be in direct reflection to their needs. Think in your customers' terms; buy, show, sell, and say things that interest them, not just what interests you. Don't forget, it is the customer that determines whether or not you succeed.

* Do you know the reasons why customers shop at your store? (service, convenience, quality, price).
* Do you seek suggestions from your best customers on ways you can boost business?
* Do you use a store questionnaire to aid you in determining your customers' needs?
* Do you ever try to re-establish lost or inactive customers?

5. Keep Good Financial Records

If you don't know where your money is going, it will soon be gone. The "game of business" is played with computers -- and the score is evaluated in dollars and cents. Good financial records are like the instruments on an airplane, they keep you posted of your height, direction, and speed. Without them you're flying blind with no controls to guide you to your destination. If you know how much you're spending, buying and selling, you can take control and make your business more money.

* Have you computerized your business to streamline everyday tasks and business procedures?
* Do you use sales forecasts, expense sheets, and financial statements on regular basis?
* Do you evaluate your operating expenses on a regular basis?

6. Manage Your Cash

It doesn't matter how unique your store is, your business can't survive without cash flow. Cash is the lifeblood of your business. The money coming into or out of your store is the vital component that keeps your business financially healthy. A monthly Cash Flow Statement shows the amount of money at the start of a period and then shows how much cash was received from various sources and the reasons it was paid out. If you budget wisely and know the interval of your monthly income and expenses, you won't have to worry about running out of money.

* Watch your monthly overhead and operating expenses ratios
* Make a budget and follow an open-to-buy plan to eliminate overbuying
* Buy closer to the selling season to minimize the risk of making a bad buy
* Don't accept deliveries you can't use or arrive after the completion date

7. Use Sound Management Practices

As store owner, you are also a manager. This means knowing how to run your business from the top to the bottom. You have to make decisions, offer customer service, manage time and resources, and know how to merchandise and run the business better than anyone working for you. Value your employees, they're your most valuable asset. Train your employees and provide them with the confidence and skills to do their jobs better. Give your employees the opportunity for growth, treat them fairly, pay them what they're worth, and they will help make your business successful.

* Do you train your employees to service and work with customers in a professional manner?
* Do you have a program to reward your employees for their extra efforts and innovative ideas?
* Do you empower employees to make important decisions, even if it means losing money?

8. Develop A Distinctive Image

Your image is important and links all the areas of your business together. It is the reality of your customers' perception of your store name, location, appearance, building, landscaping, entrance, floors, doors, counters, dressing rooms, rest rooms, products, prices, visual merchandising, signs, window displays, business cards, invoices, newsletters, advertising material, customer service, and anything else that relates to your business. Right or wrong, your image can be a "make it or break it" situation.

* Is your business distinctive and does your merchandise fit into a niche that competitors don't have?
* Do you use newsletters to remind customers of the products or services you provide?
* Do you implement proven concepts and formulas of other successful retail firms?
* Do you grade your store's location every year in regards to appearance and accessibility?

9. Control Your Inventory

The function of your inventory is to generate sales. All retail stores need to manage inventory. It is your money sitting on a shelf and represents a large portion of your business investment. The small retailer who merely watches the stores shelves can't maintain a proper balance between the right amount of merchandise and probable customer demand. That retailers buying and selling will suffer through lack of information concerning color, size, trends, and customer preferences. Without adequate control, slow-moving inventory becomes dated, shopworn, damaged, and very costly. Do you evaluate the amount of inventory you carry, and fine tune your operating expense ratios on a regular basis?

Generally, inventory controls can be summarized as follows:

* Matching the stock on hand with customers needs
* Controlling the investment in inventory
* Minimizing markdowns
* Controlling shortages
* Improving purchasing procedures

10. Buy and Price For Profit

To fully understand the nature of retailing, one must start with the concept that the original price of your merchandise is nothing more than a temporary estimate of what the customer is willing to spend. Most stores use a "keystone" markup that applies to their product or service. What they lack is a pricing strategy based on an item-by-item calculation for regular, promotional, and off-price merchandise. To boost sales, retailers must focus on items, price, and efficiency and by countering with lots of store celebrations, glamour and fun. To become more competitive, attend trade shows, join buying groups, and seek out manufacturer discounts that allow you to purchase merchandise at below wholesale prices. By offering the new price-conscious consumer better values, you'll be able to: attract more customers, improve your average sales transaction and offer customers more opportunities to visits your store.

* Do you test different aspects for promoting business: new offers, new items, new prices?
* Do you identify different vendor performance, mark-up, and turnover?
* Do you use a system for tracking those products that are your best-sellers?
* Have you tried to increase sales by offering better prices, more value, or add-ons?

11. Learn From The Pros

It takes experience to master the skills of running a business. First, you must learn How, Who, What, Where, When, How Much, and How Often to market and advertise to profitably promote your business. Second, how to quickly manage and adjust to the ups and downs of the seasonal profit cycles of your business which include: inventory, overbuying, markdowns, turnover, timing, deliveries, expenses, and projected sales. It's your money, so with expert planning and follow-through, you will be able to insure bigger sales and higher profits. A smart approach that maximizes your overall business and financial performance, while minimizing time, effort, and risk.

12. Ask For Help When You Need It

Remember, getting results is what counts! With outside advice and assistance, your quest for a major process of improvement can get a major jump start. Don't be too proud to ask for help, we all need help sometimes. Qualified sources are available from your local government offices and other professional services. It is important to recognize -- what you don't know can end up costing you money, hurt the odds of success, and greatly reduce the chance of achieving your business goals. And, most importantly, you'll have all the tools you need and a wonderful piece of mind.

Why You Should Call A Consultant

By Bob Nelson

It never ceases to amaze me that most independent retailers don't ask for outside help until it is almost too late in the game. To find solutions to tough problems, you can simply tap into the right expertise and knowledge. You don't have to allow your business to be typecast in the role of an undistinguished, uninteresting, or an unprofitable struggling enterprise.

Making the right moves is essential for your survival. In today's competitive markets, there is little room for error. For some store owners, without knowing how to navigate through these fast-moving and changing times, it can be a tricky, self-destructive experience.

Just because you're the boss does not mean you know how to solve every problem that you face in your business. That's why hiring an expert may be the most profitable decision you can make to protect your future. Sensitive to your needs, the best professionals create substantial values -- one dollar spent on a consultant should ideally yield 2-3 times that in potential profits.

In fact, seasoned specialists can quickly help you turn around any of the most common and troublesome business challenges of: enhancing cash flow, boosting sales, controlling inventory, selling overstocks, implementing technology, cutting expenses, and learning how to enjoy running a business.

Frequently, because owners are overwhelmed with serious decisions and unable to pinpoint their problems, the consultants recommended solutions may not be easy to swallow. It is like going to the doctor -- you may not like to take the prescribed medicine, but it is the unique formula to heal the pain, cure the illness, and make you well again.

Just like your doctor, be sure you're willing to empower the consultant to get the job properly done. To really benefit, be prepared to listen carefully to professional advice and then act on it. That means gathering the details and information needed, getting your employees to cooperate, and having a clear understanding of the special assignment and the expectations of a good client consultant relationship.

The most common reasons that consultants are hired:

* To Provide Expertise - applying high-impact techniques and strategies with a demonstrated and proven track record for the specific situation.

* To Provide Objectivity - creating new money-making opportunities and implementing fresh ideas with an impartial viewpoint.

* To Act as a Catalyst - developing cutting-edge solutions that initiate change and overcome typically structured procedures and outdated methods.

* To Identify Problems - providing practical answers with definitive and workable solutions to the problem and its symptoms.

* To Instruct - offering ongoing advice, assistance, coaching, trouble-shooting, wealth-building ideas, and marketing support to help ensure your success.

* To Provide Team Work - having a dynamic group to focus on the essential skills and series of multi-purpose phases to take your business to new heights.

* To Act as a Hatchet man - being used as the scapegoat in making decisions and eliminating obstacles needed for a change that may not be well received by others.

* To Provide Influence - discovering well established resources for quality name brands offprice merchandise, debt management, inventory management, and other related retail services.

* To Oversee Business Operations - assisting with the important tasks of planning, merchandising, advertising, and overall marketing strategy.

* To Optimize Performance - with a breakthrough strategy approach you'll be able to maximize your overall business and financial performance, while minimizing effort, expense and risk!

If you learn to make your business more stimulating and enjoyable with an inviting environment, people will prefer buying from you instead of your competitors. Even if you are in the final stages of operation and like most resourceful retailers who feel they have an obligation for an orderly disposal, a consultant can develop a successful exit strategy.

Remember, if you're not satisfied with the results you've been getting, and if you keep on doing what you have always been doing, nothing is ever going to change! So, whether your business is doing well now or starting to slide, a winning combination can provide a successful switch to make it easier for you to succeed.

Because of the emotional and sometimes difficult decisions that must be made, the smart owner understands the crucial difference and importance of having fresh ideas with an impartial business position. With expert advice and assistance, you'll be able to uncover hidden assets and take advantage of the many overlooked opportunities to maximize bottom line results.

Advice You Can Bank On *by Margie Johnson of SHOP TALK*

Mention going to the bank to a specialty store retailer and the immediate reaction may be one of fear, anxiety, or intimidation. As I work with specialty retailers, I emphasize that in this turbulent economic time a good banking relationship is one of utmost importance, and that we must work through these negative feelings. The first and most important step is a frequent, open line of communication with your banker. Don't let the bank or the people in it intimidate you. Remember, bankers are human despite rumors of the contrary.

Establish a great banking relationship by proving competence – this will ultimately earn confidence and respect from your banker and will put you in a more favorable position to ask for money, terms, or just advice when you need it. Outlined below are several points I encourage all retailers to practice to insure a healthy, ongoing banking relationship.

(1) *Don't wait until you need something to communicate with your banker.* Bankers are very tuned in to the high failure rate of small specialty stores. Try to schedule quarterly meetings to keep your banker updated about what you are doing. This should be a brief 15-20 minute overview that includes a copy of your recent financial statement. Include in this review examples of your advertising and direct marketing efforts. Earn your banker's respect by openly discussing the current industry problems. Let them know you are aware of certain pitfalls and advise them of your plans to avoid these problems.

(2) *Invite your banker to visit the store a few times a year.* During this visit, let them know how you manage your inventory. Learn to speak the "numbers" of inventory; turnover, maintained markup, etc. These topics will always get their attention. A banker will be impressed with your strategy of not tying too much or too little of your capital in inventory.

(3) *Keep commitments to the bank exactly as scheduled.* Carefully study repayment possibilities when establishing a line of credit or a loan. It's better to underestimate your abilities and stretch the repayment schedule a little longer than to overestimate your repayment terms and have to call for an extension.

(4) *If your personal account is with the same bank, keep it in order, too.* In a small business, it is closely related and highly scrutinized.

A good banking relationship is a valuable asset. Build and nurture your relationship with your banker. Proceed as though you are partners, both striving to make the business successful. Try to make them feel as though they are a part of your team and keep them excited about the things you are doing. Call or write your banker today and tell them something positive you are doing in your business. Nothing makes a banker happier than to see the bank's money helping make money and to feel part of the success!

(Margie Johnson is a veteran retailer with 30 years of hands-on experience. If you are interested in SHOP TALK service, call Margie at (757) 491-1411.)

Detecting Counterfeit Currency:
"What You Need to Know to Protect Your Profits!"
by...Debbie Allen "The Retail Motivator"

Two former U.S. Secret Service agents say the new $20 bill released this past year for circulation will be counterfeited on computers and color copiers and successfully passed to unsuspecting cash handlers. The loss to business, despite the bill's new anti-counterfeit features, will be in the hundreds of millions of dollars, they predict. The new anti-counterfeiting designs do not scare off the casual copier, and if cash handlers are untrained, they will be fooled over and over again.

The $20 denomination is the most commonly used in daily business and is the bill most dispensed by automated teller machines.

Retail businesses and banks do not place a high priority on detecting counterfeit bills because they believe the newly designed bills will prevent fraud. That is frustrating because they have been lulled into thinking the problem is not serious, but they're losing millions.

New technology is the culprit in the several hundred million dollars worth of counterfeit money produced annually in the United States. With the explosion of cheap color copiers, scanners, computers, and printers, counterfeiting has moved to an age in which students and grandmothers can run off a few untraceable bucks as needed.

Design changes since 1996 on $100, $50, and $20 bills include larger and off-center portraits, security threads, and water-marks. But, these measures will not thwart copy machine counterfeiting because the fraud artist knows that the average person does not take the time to learn about detection of bogus bills. Counterfeiters love an easy target, and the last person holding the counterfeit is the loser!

Since 1990, the amount of counterfeit U.S. currency passed to the public has more than tripled (hundreds of millions of dollars annually), and experts predict dramatic increases will continue because of technology and lack of public knowledge about counterfeit detection, specially at points of sales by cash handlers.

These two Secret Service agents have produced a 20-minute video on detecting counterfeit cash, which reveals all the tricks-of-the-trade and what to do about it. The tape is easy-to-follow with visuals and provides information based on hours of reseat by the Secret Service.

This is valuable information that you and your staff needs to know to protect your profits! Order your tape today and have your next staff meeting viewing and discussing how to protect yourself from this growing crime spree.

(Call Debbie Allen "The Retail Motivator", at (800) 359-4544, fax (602) 948-7487, or e-mail dallen7001@aol.com, to order your tape, "Detecting Counterfeit Currency: A Retailer's Guide Video" and counterfeit detector pen for just $29.95.)

The Retail Concept of Cross Merchandising

Gift Retailers cry, *"Give me more - more- more!"*

The *hot* new phrase in retailing, *cross merchandising* simply means your store is carrying a larger and more unusual cross-section of items than ever before. Do not confuse this with trying to be everything to everybody. Instead, this form of merchandising is adding different items that your current customer already needs and wants and is already buying somewhere else. In a sense by cross merchandising you are making their life much simpler and easier by allowing them to purchase "all" those desired items in one spot. Such as what apparel retailers have most recently done in gifts. Many ladies and mens apparel shops have added complete lines of gift items to their inventory and are currently enjoying the profits from these ventures.

Recent holidays have been a tremendous success season for the gift industry as a whole, and for those clothing stores who jumped on that band wagon early. Everything from lotions, perfumes, frames, clocks, flags, stationary, and even toys (TY Beanie Babies have taken over specialty shops) and have added diversity to store inventories and created higher sales volumes.

Now it is gift retailer's turn to *"turn about fair play,"* in that most specialty gift stores are including more and more fashion accessories in their merchandise mix. It's a natural progression.

When attending shows, enjoy shopping the apparel merchandise center as well, without an additional expense of another market trip. Many apparel showrooms are open every week day of the year which would allow a gift shop owner access to this merchandise at any time. Many have catalogs which they will gladly mail to you.

When making the decision to increase your store inventory categories to include fashion accessories, have a plan. The items should relate to your current customer base, and require very little additional promotion and advertising. For more information on the apparel industry and markets, feel free to call my office for a free copy of my newsletter, THE FASHION ADVANTAGE.

Categories to consider:

(1) Jewelry/watches

(2) Scarves/neckwear

(3) Hats/hair goods

(4) Handbags/totes/gloves

(5) Rainwear/umbrellas

(6) Leather goods & belts

Additional Requirements:

(1) Cash Flow/Finances

(2) New Display Materials

(3) More Inventory Space

(4) Extra Buying Time

(5) Additional Staff Education

(6) New Product Knowledge

A word of caution: A new and different category can seem very exciting, BUT be careful not to lose sight of the true mission of your business. Do not let the *fun* of these new goodies overwhelm your inventory or cause your other categories to suffer.

Are You Missing The Trees?
How Much Can We Really Grow Our Business?
By Rick Segel

When we look at all the things we spend money on in our business, the biggest black hole is advertising. Most of our expenses are either fixed or vary with our sales volume. For example, rent is generally a fixed expense. Packaging costs will vary with usage, i.e., the more sales, the more bags we use.

The two biggest controllable costs are still advertising and labor costs. I'll save labor for another article. The focus here will be on our attitude about advertising. That's right - attitude. Not gimmicks or tricks. Not some new fangled way to market ourselves. Not ways to save some money on radio time or new innovative ways to gather names for our mailing list. This is about how we look and feel about advertising.

Most of my work today is with independent business people and many are located in downtown areas. I keep on asking myself why are some retailers successful while others are not? What is the magic pill - that magic touch that makes some succeed beyond their belief? For the last 25 years, my answer was pat and simple. I would say it's a combination of many things: the merchandise, someone's ability to buy better, the look of the store, the salespeople, the location, pricing, etc. My response was easy. The real merchant does so many things right. I would use the old hackneyed expression - retail is detail.

But I've changed my mind, I think that there is a silver bullet. It is our image. What is the feel of your store? What do we project to the general public? I have observed the phenomenal growth and rebirth of Abercombie & Fitch. What did they do? They recognized their market and did everything to romance that market. They stand for something. It's not low prices, and certainly not their sales. They invented a market and romanced it with expensive shopping bags that actually show the type of customer that buys the clothes. They take extra markup but no one seems to care, because they want the look, that image, and that feel.

So what does all that have to do with our attitude toward advertising? EVERYTHING. Image advertising builds business. Yes, it focuses on tomorrow, not today. But if we plan our tomorrow, the today will take care of themselves. After all, this approach is easier. Why worry about endless sales? Worry about building your image, which becomes your brand, which builds your business.

This is why Nike runs image ads. Why General Electric brings good things to life. Why Nordstrom's has a flair. And Hallmark is all about people. That is why Pontiac sells excitement and the status advertising of American Express built that brand. That is why the new VW Bug is tapping into that nostalgia feeling. They are not concerned with the buy one/get one half price thinking. They are concerned with the look and image. Years ago, we called it institutional advertising. Many of these retailers that did that actually created institutions. Yet, so many of us concern ourselves with the everyday and forget that building an image or better yet, creating the benefit to our customers, will make our businesses grow.

Take some of the hard sell out of your advertising. Create the mood, and watch the tomorrows become profitable today!

(Rick Segel can reached at Rick Segel & Associates, (781) 272-9995, (781) 272-9996 fax.)

Where Can I Find . . .?

This is probably the phrase I hear most when I answer the phone each day. If the person on the other end of the line is a subscriber to my newsletter <u>FASHION ADVANTAGE</u>, I am happy to try to answer. Even if they're not on our list, I'll usually answer anyway, and then attempt to convince the caller to subscribe. After all, just that one little tidbit probably paid for the newsletter cost for an entire year.

The information I dispense comes from a combination of research, and over thirty years of experience in the business. Most of the resources, manufacturers, suppliers, consultants, etc. are ones I have used in my store, or people who come highly recommended from other store owners. A lot of the information has been shared in networking sessions throughout the country with successful retailers from California to Connecticut. As I advised you in past chapters, networking is the best way to gain the experience and expertise you need. Profit and learn from others. It is far less expensive and painful to benefit from the mistakes of others, than to make them all yourself.

<u>CONSIGNMENT COMPANIES</u>:

Often store owners are looking for manufacturers or suppliers who will offer current new merchandise on consignment. It is very profitable if you can find someone who has items that will fit into your inventory mix for consignment, but that should be your criteria for selection: *The merchandise should compliment and blend in with your regular stock.* If it does, you're very lucky; if it doesn't you can possibly hurt the reputation and creditability of your store. Most consignment dealers operate on a percentage basis, offering a no-risk policy. If you don't sell it, you don't pay for it. They take it back - no questions asked. Usually, you make the same percentage of profit regardless of the markdown, if approved by the consignor. Be careful to read fully any agreement you sign. If it sounds too good to be true, it probably is. Ask for references, and *call* the references on any dealer you do business with.

The following four come highly recommended to my office by retailers:

CND Corporation is owned and operated by David Morgan, offering ladies apparel on consignment to qualifying stores. 1-888-626-6580.

Dresses Unlimited is owned and operated by Murray Levey, and also deals in ladies apparel and sportswear. Call 1-908-422-7993.

CINE` is a Houston-based jewelry consignment supplier for ladies specialty stores. Call 1-800-258-3327 for Allan Robin.

A.C. Fashions is located in the mid-west. Their specialty is coats. For more information, contact Melanie at 618-234-6273.

Where Can I Find . . .?

OFF PRICE MERCHANDISE:

The first place to look for off-price offerings is from your regular vendors. If you purchase merchandise at full-price from them each season you should be given the opportunity to take advantage of their season-end savings before they sell it off to discounters. But you have to ask. They are never going to just offer to give you 25% off your shipment; there is an art to off-price negotiating and buying. It takes practice, but eventually you will feel comfortable asking your sales representative and customer service reps for their special deals.

There are hundreds of companies nationwide that act as wholesalers, discounters and jobbers of merchandise. Many are listed regularly in FASHION ADVANTAGE if they are recommended by our subscribers. To find out more about these and other people in this field, call **The Off-Price Specialist Center** at 414-781-6300. They have a resource guide and a magazine for this industry.

STORE OPENING SERVICES:

If you want a company to help you open a store from start to finish, I suggest you call **LIBERTY FASHIONS, INC**. They offer everything in a complete package from fixtures to inventory to consulting advice. This turn-key operation covers all categories from children's to women's to men's and gifts and housewares - even $1.00 stores. No where else will you find such a complete program for establishing your own business with the hassle and headaches. Call 1-800-443-8407.

"JUNKMAN" JOBBER

If you're new to the fashion industry, that term will confuse and amaze you. If you're a veteran you are probably squealing with delight. A junkman is the term used for the person who buys end-of-the-season leftovers. Yes, the one who pays you money to carry your "junk" away. No matter how much it costs you up-front, when the selling season is over, the item is worthless if it hasn't sold. Many stores will markdown to 50%,60% - even 75% off, but after that I suggest you just give up. There is no reason to destroy the atmosphere and reputation of your business by continuing to have old, out-of-season inventory hanging on an unattractive rack. Your regular price business will suffer.

Some stores will pack and store merchandise from one season to the next. Again, I feel this is a mistake. If your customers didn't like it when it was brand new, why will they want it a year later? Bite the bullet, take an inventory, calculate your loss, and sell it to a junkman. Cash in your hand is worth much more than old hangers in the stockroom. Take the money and reinvest in something that will sell. Remember $5.00 worth of merchandise that is turning three times a year far exceeds $50 in storage generating no profits. It's costing you money in storage space and taxes.

There are many of these dealers across the country, but nationwide the only one I have had a good experience with is **CLOTHES-OUT**. They will pay for old inventory, and you can start again fresh and new. For information, call Helen at **CLOTHES -OUT**, 1-937-898-2975.

TAX-DEDUCTIONS FOR MERCHANDISE

If you are against marking down merchandise and/or selling it to a junkman, your other option is to donate leftover inventory to a charity. The Goodwill, Red Cross, homeless shelters and other organizations will gladly accept your merchandise for their charities.

Talk to your acccountant and see what documentation is necessary to legally receive a tax deduction for these donations. It is very important to have the proper forms and inventory appraisal.

STORE CREDIT CARDS

Printing your own store credit cards or identification cards for Frequent Buyer Programs can be less expensive than you think. Contact **Vanguard** at **(800) 323-7432** for more information.

HOLIDAY LISTINGS:

"Chase's Annual Events" is a huge national directory of every holiday you could ever imagine. This list will keep you in promotions for the rest of your life. The day-to-day calendar helps you plan special occasions and events for your business. Almost 800 pages of information, it is available from **NTC/Contemporary Publishing Group**, 4255 W. Touchy Avenue, Lincolnwood, Il. 60646-1975. You can call **(847) 679-5500** or fax **(847) 679-6388**. Price for Year 2000 issue is $59.95 + S/H.

PRIVATE LABEL PRODUCTS:

Lotions, soaps, candles, sachets - everything you ever needed for a bath & body department as well as advertising and marketing tools for your store. Call **Roland Neal** at **(800) 749-5909**.

ADVERTISING SPECIALTY PRODUCTS:

For those t-shirts, tote bags and other specialty items, I suggest you try a local vendor first. Remember these people are your potential customers as well as friends. Try to deal or barter with them first. If this fails, try **Newton Manufacturing (515) 792-4121** with agents nationwide or Specialities at **(412) 834-4428**. They have a neat little clothes hanger magnet you can give away.

SCRATCH-OFF GAME PIECES:

Call Scratch- It Promotions **(800) 966-WINS** for these and other promotional game ideas.

RMSA National Headquarters

For information on how they can help you: **(800) 727-7672** or www.forseon.com/RMSA

Where Can I Find . . .?

FASHION GUIDES - EARRING BOOKS - FASHION CALENDARS

My office **(800) 221-8615** publishes wonderful 16 page booklets which make perfect handouts for style shows, as well as great gift-with-purchase items. Each year we create a fashion calendar for you to use as a holiday gift for your VIP customers. These products start at less than a dollar. We are constantly adding new products like these for your customer service and promotional needs. New product in the development stage is greeting cards for retailers.

APPAREL SOURCE GUIDE

For our newsletter subscribers, we have this book on hand for research; just call. For others, if you wish to buy **The National Register of Apparel Manufacturers** (Women's & Children); it is available through Marche Publishing **(800) 347-2589.** The cost is $159; $294 to include men's.

FORTUNE COOKIE PROMOTION

Customized fortune cookies and boxes, tailored to fit your sales promotion for your individual store. Call Van at **Fresh Approach Marketing (817) 731-8932** for sample and details.

SMALL BUSINESS COLLECTION

Rick Segel offers many audio tapes, videos, books, workbooks and manuals on successfully running a retail store. Call **Rick Segel & Associates** at **(718) 272-9996.**

BUYING OFFICES

There are many buying offices around the country for every category imaginable. I work with and recommend **Billye Little & Associates** in Dallas. Call for Karen at **(214) 634-0691.**

RETAIL PROMOTIONS

Bob Nelson of **POWER RETAILING** is the person you want to call for help in this field. He has wonderful references. Call **(800) 399-1980** for a no obligation free consultation.

Useful and Informative Trade Magazines

A successful retailer is one who stays on top of the latest trends and market events. As a busy store owner I realize you don't have a lot of time for reading, but you do need knowledge about your industry. Here are a few to choose from. Share them with your employees. Assign each a book or a magazine to read. Ask them to highlight sections they find of interest for future reference.

ACCENT - 100 Wells Avenue, Newton, Ma. 02159 - 617-964-5100
Annual subscription rate is $38.00 Topic: Fashion Accessories

ACCESSORIES - 185 Madison Avenue, New York, N. Y. 10016 -
212-686-4412 Annual subscription rate is $38.00 Topic: Fashion Accessories

APPAREL NEWS - 110 E. 9th Street #A-777, L.A. Ca. 90079 - 213-627-3737
Annual newspaper subscription (52 issues) $36.00 Topic: Fashion (wholesale)

BY DESIGN - P.O. Box 10384, Phoenix, Az. 850634 - 888-391-9877
Six issues per year for $29.95   Topic: Gift basket design

CHILDREN'S BUSINESS, 7 W. 34th St., New York, N.Y. 10001 - 800-360-1700
Annual subscription rate: $39.00   Topic: Children's

COUNTRY BUSINESS, Box 420839, Palm Coast, Fl. 32142
Annual subscription rate: free in the U.S. - just ask

DNR (Daily News Record) 7 W. 34th St., New York, N. Y. 10001 - 800-360-1700
Annual subscription rate daily newspaper: $62.00 Topic: Men's wholesale

DALLAS FASHION UPDATE, 725 Lakeview, Lucas, TX., 75002 - 214-727-5266
Free publication available during all five Dallas women's fashion markets

FOOTWEAR NEWS, 7 W. 34th St., New York, N. Y. 10001 - 800-360-1700
Annual subscription rate newspaper: $62.00 Topic; Footwear business

GBS GIFT & STATIONERY BUSINESS, 600 Harrison St., San Francisco, Ca.94107
415-905-2200   Annual subscription rate: $45.00 Topic: Gifts

GIFTS & DEC, 345 Hudson St., New York, N. Y. 10014 - 212-519-7200
Annual subscription rate: $42.00   Topic: Gifts

GIFTS & TABLEWARES, 1450 Don Mills Rd., Don Mills, Ont. M3B2X7
800-268-7742 - Canadian magazine - call for U.S. rate

Annual subscription rate: $36.00   Topic: Gifts

HOME ACCENTS TODAY, Box 2754, High Point, N.C. 27261 - 336-605-0121
Annual subscription rate: $29.95   Topic: Home decor

INTIMATE FASHION NEWS, 307 Fifth Ave., New York, N.Y. 10016 -
212-679-6677 Annual subscription rate: $25.00 Topic: Lingerie/ intimate apparel

MR, 185 Madison Avenue, New York, N. Y. 10016 - 212-686-4412
Annual subscription rate: $24.00 Topic: Mens apparel (wholesale)

NICHE Magazine, 3000 Chestnut Avenue, Baltimore, Md. 21211 -410-235-5116
Annual subscription rate: $17.97 (4 issues)   Topic: gift and craft industry

OUTERWEAR, 19 W. 21st St., New York, N. Y. 10010 - 212-727-1210
Annual subscription rate: $80.00   Topic: Outerwear (wholesale)

PAGEANTRY, 1855 W. State Road, #434, Longwood, Fl. 32750 - 407-260-2262
Annual subscription rate: $38.00 Topic: Formals, pageants (retail)

RETAIL NEWS, 265 Yorkland Blvd. #301, North York, On. M2J1S5
416-385-8888 - Canadian gift magazine, call for U.S. rate

SCREEN PRINTING, 407 Gilbert Avenue, Cincinnati, Ohio 45202 - 1-800-421-1321
Fax - 513-421-6110   Annual subscription rate: $39.00   Topic: Screen printing

SPECIALTY RETAIL, 293 Washington St., Norweil, Ma. 02061 - 800-936-6297
Annual subscription rate: $49.95   Topic: Retail business

STORES, the magazine of the National Retail Federation - 202-626-8146
Free to all NRF members, $49.00 annually for non-members   Topic: retail business

SWIM FASHION QUARTERLY, 414 N. Scottsdale Rd #316, Scottsdale, Az 85281
Annual subscription rate: $33.00   Topic: Swimwear (wholesale)

TACK 'N TOGS, 12400 Whitewater Dr. #160, Minnetonka, Mn. 55343 612-930-4390
Annual subscription rate: $25.00   Topic: Westernwear, tack

VISUAL MERCHANDISING & STORE DESIGN, 407 Gilbert Avenue, Cincinnati,
Ohio 45202 - 1-800-421-1321, Annual subscription rate: $39.00   Topic: visual design

Newspapers

WOMEN'S WEAR DAILY, 7 W. 34th St., New York, N.Y. 10001 - 800-360-1700
Annual newspaper subscription daily rate: $260.00 (Specials are offered frequently)

National Industry Newsletters

FASHION ADVANTAGE, P. O. Box 977, Amite, La. 790422 - 800-221-8615
Annual subscription rate: $129.00 Topic: Apparel retail, edited and written by T. J. Reid, this newsletter was founded in 1989 and is the oldest of its type in the industry. (T.J. Reid was formerly a contributor to Specialty Store Bulletin which closed in the mid-80's.) **FASHION ADVANTAGE** is geared to small to medium specialty stores who sell women's apparel and accessories. It is very targeted and niche specific because it offers a networking opportunity for retailers who share the same interests. Articles are on topics including buying, employee relations, visuals, trend reports, sales training, promotions, and hot items lists. Money-back guarantee offer; subscription price is refunded if you are not satisfied.

WWD SPECIALTY STORES, 7 W. 34th St., New York, N Y 10001 - 212-630-4199
Annual subscription rate: $299.00   Topic: Apparel/gift retail, published by Fairchild Publications. **WWD Specialty Stores** is geared to all specialty retail including gifts, women's apparel, and men's apparel. Topics covered include all business related subjects including advertising, employee training, customer service and promotions..

GIFT BEAT, 145 Woodland Avenue, Westwood, N.J. 07675 - 1-800-358-7177
Annual subscription rate: $129.00   Topic: Gift industry trends. This is a monthly publication to guide you in ordering decisions and spotlight new lines. Provides a network for gift retailers.

Subscription Service

Diamond Publications, 29832 Roscoe Blvd. #104, Canoga Park, Ca. 91306
818-700-6920 , offers a complete line of trade magazine subscriptions and books for the apparel and gift industry (wholesale & retail). Most of the items listed on the last few pages can be purchased directly through Diamond Publications. They accept all major credit cards and ship at once.

Business/Office/Store Supplies

It is very easy to get caught up in the excitement of gift or fashion retail and ignore the basics of supplies for managing your business. Make a list of basic supplies you need - include tags, pricing guns, labels, stationery, business cards, invoices, order forms, envelopes, shipping supplies, gift card enclosures, gift certificates, mailing labels, mailing tap, tape guns, bookkeeping systems, promotional products, payroll system, payroll cards, signs, banners, boxes, bags, tissue, steamer, giftwrap, and the list goes on and on and on.

If you can't find these items at a reasonable price or products are unavailable within your area, these are companies which I, and many of my newsletter subscribers use and recommend. I feel confident in referring them for your supply needs:

CHEAP FURNITURE Yes, that's really their name. Cheap enough for store displays, but good enough to sell. Call for catalog. 1-800-533-2527

THE BUSINESS BOOK Call 1-800-558-0220 for their catalog of labels, stationery, forms, ad specialities (great full color birthday cards), office supplies.

GIFT BOX CORPORATION OF AMERICA Call 1-800-GIFT BOX or fax (201) 933-5316 for catalog of excellent gift boxes.

NASHVILLE WRAPS Call 1-800-547-9727 for bags, boxes, cards, cello, giftwrap, tissue and other wrapping supplies. They offer free freight, and satisfaction guaranteed.

PAPER DIRECT Call 1-800-A-PAPERS for a catalog of wonderful designs in paper to use for mailers and newsletters.

RAPID FORMS Call 1-800-257-8354 for their catalog of labels, forms, tags, ad specialities, pricing guns, binders, register supplies, etc.

RETAIL EDGE Call 1-800-777-2445 for some really great promotions. Terrific scratch-offs, postcards, etc. For small specialty stores, gift & apparel related. Website www.retail-edge.com

R & M (Russell Miller) Call 1-800-231-9600 for their catalog of a full range of retail merchandising products from tags to labels to display items, sign kits, and more.

SOUTHWEST FIXTURE DISPLAY Call 800-442-7048 for catalog information on greats store fixtures and display items. Visit their website is swfdc.com.

VIKING OFFICE PRODUCTS Call 1-800-421-1222 for their discount buyers guide and to be put on their catalog list. They send a catalog monthly of their special office supply bargains. They are known for their free and fast delivery on any order over $25. Offers 30 day credit.

National Trade Associations

Keep this information handy. All of these organizations offer brochures, information and assistance which can be helpful. These are the national headquarters for the groups:

Accessories Council
350 Fifth Avenue #912
New York, New York 10118
(212) 947-1135

Acrylic Council
1285 Avenue of the Americas
New York, New York 10019
(212) 554-4041

American Apparel Manufacturers Assoc.
2500 Wilson Blvd. # 301
Arlington, Va. 22201
(703) 524-1864

American Craft Council
72 Spring Street
New York, New York 10012
(212) 274-0630

American Gem Association
2050 Stemmons #181
Dallas, Texas 75207
(214) 742-4367

American Jewelry Design Council
10 Bleeker Street #1A
New York, New York 10012
(212) 673-0643

American Watch Association
P.O. Box 464
Washington, D. C. 20044
(703) 759-3377

Apparel Industries Chamber of Commerce
570 7th Avenue
New York, New York 10018
(212) 354-0907

Apparel Marketing Group
16 West 27th Street
New York, New York 10010
(212) 627-0590

Apparel Retailers of America
2011 I Street NW #250
Washington, D. C. 20006
(202) 347-1932

Belt Association
145 West 45th Street #800
New York, New York 10036
(212) 398-5400

Cotton, Inc.
1370 Avenue of the Americas
New York, N.Y. 10019
(212) 506-586-1070

Council of Fashion Designers (CFDA)
1412 Broadway #2006
New York, New York 10018
(212) 302-1821

Direct Marketing Association
1120 Avenue of the Americas
New York, New York 10036
(212) 768-7277

Fashion Accessories Association
67 Broad Street #26
New York, New York 10004
(212) 425-0055

The Fashion Calendar
153 East 87th
New York, New York 10128
(212) 289-0420

Fashion Footwear Association
768 Fifth Avenue #17
New York, New York 10019
(212) 832-1745

Fashion Group International
597 Fifth Avenue
New York, New York 10017
(212) 593-1715

Footwear Industries of America
1420 K St.. N. W. #600
Washington, D.C. 20005
(202) 789-1420

Footwear Retailers of America
1319 F St.. NW #700
Washington, D. C. 20004

Fur Fashion Council
224 W. 30th Street
New York, New York 10010
(212) 564-5133

Gold Council
900 Third Avenue # 26
New York, New York 10022
(212) 688-0005

International Mass Retail Association
1700 N. Moore Street #2250
Arlington, Va. 22209
(703) 841-2300

International Sign Association
801 N. Fairfax #205
Alexandria, Va. 22314
(703) 836-4012

Lycra - Dupont
1430 Broadway - 4th Floor
New York, New York 10018
(212) 512-9200

Millinery Information Bureau
302 West 12th Street # C
New York, New York 10014
(212) 627-8333

Museum Store Association
501 S. Cherry Street #460
Denver, Co. 80222
(303) 329-6968

National Association of Display Industries
355 Lexington Avenue
New York, New York 10017
(212) 661-889-0727

National Assoc. of Hosiery Manufacturers
200 North Sharon Amity Road
Charlotte, N.C. 28211
(704) 365-0913

National Fashion Accessories Association
330 Fifth Avenue #206
New York, New York 10001
(212) 947-3424

National Retail Federation
325 7th Street NW #1000
Washington, D. C. 20004
(202) 783-7971

National Shoe Retailers
9861 Broken Lane Parkway
Columbia, Mod. 21046
(212) 289-0420

Naturally Texas
1720 Regal Row #118
Dallas, Texas 75235
(214) 951-9655
(214) 951-9657 fax

New York Raincoat Mfg.. Assoc.
500 Seventh Avenue
New York, New York 10018
(212) 819-1011

Off-Price Specialist Center
14040W. Capital Drive
Brookfield. Wi. 53005
(414) 781-6300

Point of Purchase Advertising Inst.
1660 L Street NW - 10th Floor
Washington, D. C. 20036
(202) 530-3000

Retail Advertising & Marketing
333 N. Michigan Avenue #3000
Chicago, Il. 60601
(312) 251-7262

Specialty Advertising Assoc. International
3125 Skyway Circle N.
Irving, Tx. 75038
(214) 252-0404

Sunglass Association
49 East Avenue
Norwalk, Ct. 06851
(203) 845-9015

The Woolmark Company
330 Madison Avenue - 19th Floor
New York, N.Y. 10017
(800) 986-WOOL
(212) 557-5985 fax
website: www.woolmark.com

United Jewelry Show Assoc.
3 Davol Square # 177
Providence, R. I. 02903
(401) 331-7630

United States Watch Council, Inc.
P.O. Box 1102
Wheeling, Il. 60090
(847) 541-3941

Women's Jewelry Association
333B Rote 46 W #B201
Fairfield, N. J. 07004
(973) 575-7190

State Retail Associations

Alabama Retail Association
P. O. Box 1090
Montgomery, Al. 36102
(334) 263-5757
(334) 262-3991 fax

Arizona Retailers Association
137 E. University Drive
Mesa, Az. 85201
(602) 833-0009
(602) 833-0011 fax

Arkansas Retail Merchants Association.
1123 University Avenue #718
Little Rock, Ar. 72204
(501) 664-8680
(501) 664-6099 fax

California Retailers Association
980 9th Street #2100
Sacramento, Ca. 95814
(916) 443-1975
(916) 441-4218 fax

Colorado Retail Council
451 East 58th Avenue #412
Denver, Co. 80216
(303) 297-0657
(303) 297-0735 fax

Connecticut Retail Merchants Association
60 Forest Street
Hartford, Ct. 06105
(860) 527-1044
(860) 493-7476 fax

Delaware Retail Council, Inc.
P. O. Box 671
Wilmington, De. 19899
(302) 655-7221
(302) 654-0691 fax

The Greater Washington Board of Trade
1129 20th Street, NW #200
Washington, D.C. 20036
(202) 857-5936
(202) 223-2648 fax

Florida Retail Federation
P. O. Box 10024
Tallahassee, Fl. 32302
(904) 222-4082
(904) 561-6625

Georgia Retail Association
100 Englewood Avenue NE #1804
Atlanta, Ga. 30303
(404) 577-3435
(404) 525-0257

Retail Merchants of Hawaii
539 Cooke Street #203
Honolulu, Hi. 96813
(808) 592-4200
(808) 592-4202 fax

Idaho Retailers Association, Inc.
4980 West State St., #B
Boise, Id. 83703
(208) 853-2874
(208) 853-6671 fax

Illinois Retail Merchants Association
19 South LaSalle #300
Chicago, Il. 60603
(312) 726-4600
(312) 726-9570

Indiana Retail Council
One North Capital #430
Indianapolis, In. 46204
(317) 632-7391
(317) 632-7399 fax

Iowa Retail Federation, Inc.
P.O. Box 22040
Des Moines, Ia. 50325
(515) 270-1729
(515) 270-2903 fax

Kansas Retail Council
835 Southwest Topeka Boulevard
Topeka, Ks. 66612
(913) 357-6321
(913) 357-4732 fax

Kentucky Retail Federation, Inc.
512 Capital Avenue
Frankfort, Ky. 40601
(502) 875-1444
(502) 875-1595 fax

Louisiana Retailers Association
P. O. Box 44034
Baton Rouge, La. 70804
(225) 344-9481
(225) 383-4145 fax

Maine Merchants Association
P. O. Box 5060
Augusta, Me. 04332
(207) 623-1149
(207) 623-8377 fax

Maryland Retailers Association
171 Conduit Street
Annapolis, Md. 21401
(410) 269 - 1440
(410) 269-0325 fax

Retailers Association of Massachusetts
18 Tremont Street #1040
Boston, Ma. 02108
(617) 523-1900
(617) 523-4321 fax

Michigan Retailers Association
603 South Washington Avenue
Lansing, Mi. 48933
(517) 372-5757
(517) 372-1303 fax

Minnesota Retail Merchants Association
50 East 5th Street #208
St. Paul, Mn. 55101
(612) 227-6631
(612) 297-6260 fax

Retail Association of Mississippi
4785 I-55 North, Suite #103
Jackson, Ms. 39206
(601) 362-8900
(601) 981-5566 fax

Missouri Retailers Association
P. O. Box 1336
Jefferson City, Mo. 65102
(573) 636-5128
(573) 636-6846 fax

Montana Retail Association
1537 Avenue D, Suite #320
Billings, Mt. 59102
(406) 256-1005
(406) 256-0785 fax

Nebraska Retail Federation
P. O. Box 95106
Lincoln, Ne. 68509
(402) 474-5255
(402) 474-3154 fax

Retail Association of Nevada
305 North Carson Street, #203
Carson City, Nv. 89701
(702) 882-1700
(702) 882-1713 fax

Retail Association of New Hampshire
80 North Main Street
Concord, N. H. 03301
(603) 225-9748
(603) 229-0060 fax

New Jersey Retail Merchants Association
332 West State Street
Trenton, N.J. 08618
(609) 393-8006
(609) 393-8463 fax

New Mexico Retail Federation
1476 St. Francis Drive
Santa Fe, N. M. 87505
(505) 988-9615
(505) 988-9264 fax

The Retail Council of New York State
P. O. Box 1992
Albany, N.Y. 12201
(518) 465-3586
(518) 465-7960 fax

North Carolina Retail Merchants Association
P.O. Box 176001
Raleigh, N.C. 27619
(919) 787-9520
(919) 783-7342 fax

North Dakota Retail Association
P.O. Box 1956
Bismarck, N.D. 58502
(701) 223-3370
(701) 223-5004 fax

Ohio Council of Retail Merchants
50 West Broad Street #2020
Columbus, Ohio 43215
(614) 221-7833
(614) 221-7020 fax

Oklahoma Retail Merchants Association
2519 Northwest 23rd Street #101
Oklahoma City, Ok. 73107
(405) 947-5503
(405) 946-9203

Oregon Retail Council
P. O. Box 12519
Salem, Or. 97309
(503) 588-0050
(503) 588-0052 fax

Pennsylvania Retailers Association
224 Pine Street
Harrisburg, Pa. 17101
(717) 233-7976
(717) 236-1234 fax

Rhode Island Retail Federation
30 Exchange Terrace
Providence, R.I. 02903
(401) 621-6106
(401) 751-2434 fax

South Carolina Merchants Association
1735 St. Julien Place #304
Columbia, S. C. 29204
(803) 765-0477
(803) 765-2213 fax

South Dakota Retailers Association
P. O. Box 368
Pierre, S. D. 57501
(605) 224-5050
(605) 224-2059 fax

Tennessee Council of Retail Merchants
530 Church Street #200
Nashville, Tn. 37219
(615) 256-4771
(615) 256-4773 fax

Texas Retailers Association
504 West 12th Street
Austin, Tx. 78701
(512) 472-8261
(512) 474-5011 fax

Utah Retail Merchants Association
1578 West 1700 South #200
Salt Lake City, Ut. 84104
(801) 973-9583
(801) 972-8712 fax

Vermont Retail Association
P. O. Box 688
Essex Junction, Vt. 05453
(802) 879-6999
(802) 879-6419 fax

Virginia Retail Merchants Association
Old City Hall #315
1001 East Broad Street
Richmond, Va. 23219
(804) 649-0789
(804) 644-8762 fax

Washington Retail Association
P. O. Box 2227
Olympia, Wa. 98507
(360) 943-9198
(360) 943-1032 fax

West Virginia Retailers Association
240 Capital Street #610
Charleston, W.V. 25301
(304) 342-1183
(304) 342-1471 fax

Wisconsin Merchants Federation
30 Mifflin Street #310
Madison, Wi. 53703
(608) 257-3541
(608) 257-8755 fax

Wyoming Retail Merchants Association
211 West 19th #201
Cheyenne, Wy. 82001
(307) 634-7768
(307) 632-0249 fax

Bureau of Wholesale Representatives Directory
Updated List 1999

Most regional shows are directed by members of the Bureau of Wholesale Representatives. The following list will show you the affiliate in your area. Call their offices for information on show dates and locations nearest you. Many of these offices sponsor more than one show or sponsor shows in different states (i.e. Cotton States Fashion Exhibitors listed in Memphis, Tennessee actually has their show in Tunica, Mississippi). If you are in doubt about any particular group, call the national office:

Bureau of Wholesale Sales Representatives
Suite #700, 1100 Spring Street - NW
Atlanta, Georgia 30309-2829
(800) 877-1808
Website: http.//bwsr.com

Apparel Guild
Marilyn Potash, Show Contact
2655 Park Circle
East Meadow, NY 11554
(516) 735-1595
(516)735-1595 fax

Arkansas Fashion Exhibitors
Darrell Wallraven, Show Contact
1 Twin Pine Place
Little Rick, Ar. 72209-5646
(501) 455-0494
(501) 455-5851 fax

Association of Visual Merchandise Reps
Thomas S. Raguse, Show Contact
307 Cove Creek Lane
Houston, Tx. 77042-1023
(713) 782-5533
(713) 785-1114 fax

Billings Market Association, Inc.
Shawna Valentine, Show Contact
P.O. Box 80145
Billings, Mt. 59108-0145
(406) 652-6132
(406) 652-2531 fax

Birmingham Apparel Market, Inc.
Sandi Garrett, Show Contact
4004 Dolly Ridge Road
Birmingham, Al. 35243
(205) 871-3305
(888) 209-7707 fax

Boot & Shoe Travelers of NY
Mary Scanton, Show Contact
50 West 34th Street
New York, N.Y. 10001
(212) 564-1069
(212) 564-0513 fax

Carolina-Virginia Fashion Exhibitors
Mike Realon, Show Contact
800 Briar Creek Road DD-511
Charlotte, N. C. 28205
(704) 376-3006
(704) 376-2833 fax

Central Western Market Association
Jan Ohlinger, Show Contact
Box 54060656
Omaha, Ne. 68154-2502
(402) 330-4572
(402) 333-1352 fax

Cotton States Fashion Exhibitors
Ricki Fife, Show Contact
5685 Mason Road
Memphis, Tn. 38120
(901) 683-0304
(901) 683-2401 fax

Denver Market Association
Jan Diede, Show Contact
451 East 58th Avenue #4287
Denver, Co. 80216
(303) 295-1334
(303) 295-1334 fax

Eastern Outdoor Reps Association
Debbie Motz, Show Contact
P.O. Box 18282
Ashville, N. C. 28814-0283
(828) 252-7956
(828) 252-0623 fax

Fashion Exhibitors of America, Inc.
Carol Shalberg, Show Contact
15068 Country Ridge Drive
Chesterfield, Mo. 63017-7663
(314) 537-1520
(314) 537-1405 fax

Golden Gate Apparel
Dianne E. Travalini, Show Contact
12925 Alcosta Blvd., #7
San Ramon, Ca. 94583
(925) 328-1122
(925) 328-1119 fax

Iowa Fashion Market, Inc.
Clara DeFino, Show Contact
P.O. Box 13404
Des Moines, Ia. 50310-0999
(515) 277-0414

Metropolitan Fashion Sportswear Exhibitors
Armand Havas, Show Contact
221 West 82nd St, Apt. 8G
New York, N.Y. 10024-5411
(212) 873-4347

Mid-Atlantic Men's & Boy's Apparel Club
Margaret Zente, Show Contact
4509 Old Court Road
Pikesville, Md. 21208
(410) 484-2752
(410 486-2081 fax

Middle Tennessee Fashion Exhibitors
Donnie L. Weiss, Show Contact
P.O. Box 54
Dickson, Tn. 37055
(615) 446-8004
(615) 446-5212 fax

New England Apparel Club, Inc.
Rhonda Goldberg, Show Contact
26 Darmouth Street #130
Westwood, Ma. 02090-2630
(781) 326-9223
(781) 326-6892 fax

New Orleans Fashion Association
Dan Morris, Show Contact
1037 Minden Avenue
Kenner, La. 70062
(504) 461-5196

Northwest Salesman's Assn../Upper
Midwest Men's Apparel Club
Joan Peterson, Show Contact
4052 Hyatt Merchandise Mart
Minneapolis, Mn. 55403
(800) 272-6972
(612) 333-5226 fax

Pacific Coast Travelers, Inc.
Jan Morrow, Show Contact
110 East 9th Street, C-640
Los Angeles, Ca. 90079
(213) 622-0761
(213) 629-4413 fax

Pacific Northwest Apparel Association, Inc.
Mary Bishop, Show Contact
2601 Elliot, #4123
Seattle, Was. 98121-1326
(206) 728-6622
(206) 728-1797 fax

Phoenix Women's Apparel Association
Joyce Cardova, Show Contact
4816 E. Marilyn
Scottsdale, Az. 85254
(602) 494-7203
(602) 494-7203 fax

Pittsburgh Fashion Mart
Bernie Hanlon, Show Contact
105 Mall Boulevard
Monroeville, Pa. 15146-2227
(412) 856-5010
(412) 856-4604 fax

Sales Representatives of Dallas, Inc.
Bette Hamilton, Show Contact
P.O. Box 586454 - Mart #2B35
Dallas, Texas 75258
(214) 631-0821
(214) 631-3546 fax

Salt Lake Fashion Exhibitors
Sherry Long, Show Contact
230 West 200 South #2301
Salt Lake City, Utah 84101-1101
(801) 531-6699
(801) 575-2101 fax

San Francisco Children's Wear Association
Bill Kahn, Show Contact
888 Brannan Street #3070
San Francisco, Ca. 94103
(415) 621-9930
(415) 621-9932 fax

Southeastern Travelers Exhibitors, Inc.
Dot Bissell, Show Contact
1100 Spring St. NW #700
Atlanta, Ga. 30309
(800) 948-6743 #119
(404) 870-7601 fax

Southern Apparel Exhibitors
Donna Skinner, Show Contact
7220 N. W. 36th St., #309
Miami, Fl. 33166
(305) 718-4320
(305) 718-4323 fax

United Southwest Children's Org.
Frank Ziebell, Show Contact
AM Box 585675 - AM Room 3B55
Dallas, Texas 75258
(214) 630-2384
(214) 630-2391 fax

West Coast Western Market
Despina Kreatsoulas, Show Contact
4208 N. Freeway Blvd., #106
Sacramento, Ca. 95834
(916) 929-1551
(916) 929-0386 fax

Western & English Sales Association
Toni High, Show Contact
451 East 58th Avenue, #4128
Denver, Co. 80216-1404
(303) 295-1040
(303) 295-0941 fax

About the author . . .

At age 10, T.J. Reid couldn't decide between being a fashion designer and living in New York, or being a novelist, and living in New York. By age 12 she had entered both fields - working in a department store in Kentwood, Louisiana, and writing a teen column for the local paper in Kentwood, Louisiana.

She opened her own ladies apparel and gift shop in Amite, Louisiana, in her mid-twenties where she established a reputation as "one of the southwest's most outstanding retailers." (Dallas Apparel News). She was named Louisiana Retailer of the Year in 1984, Chamber of Commerce Woman of the Year, and was listed in Outstanding Young Women of America and Outstanding Women of the World, but deep down inside still longed to be a writer. She spent her days on the sales floor, but her nights at the typewriter pouring out her soul in a journal style diary of retail.

By age 45 she still was longing to take the chance of pursuing that career in journalism and heeded the advice of a friend, *"You must give up what you are for what you can become."* She closed the store in it's most prosperous year, and the long-time successful retailer evolved into a small store sage and best-selling author of America's *bible* for specialty store owners, **"What Mother Never Told Ya About Retail."**

Traveling across the country presenting seminars at market centers and trade shows, T.J. touches the lives and hearts of each person she meets. She involves herself in their problems and their successes, truly seeking to make a difference in their retail lives. Her workshops on advertising, customer service, and just basic retailing from A to Z, draw standing room only crowds of newcomers and retail veterans, all anxious to learn more from this lady who bares her soul and shares her every thought and idea to help make their business better. As Networking Director for the Dallas Market Center since the early 1990's, T.J. helps other retailers meet and connect, through regular sessions of sharing. Many ideas from retailers in these sessions make up her second book, **"52 Promotions - A Year's Worth of Profit!"**

Her **FASHION ADVANTAGE** newsletter, established in 1989 is a monthly publication for apparel store owners. Named Best Newsletter in 1998 by The National Press Women's Association, it features hot items, fashion trends and basic business information much needed in the daily life of a fashion retailer. She is a contributing writer for several trade magazines (DALLAS FASHION UPDATE, PAGEANTRY MAGAZINE, STYLE, ACCESSORIES) and has been featured in every national fashion and gift industry publication.

When not on the road at markets, speaking at women's events or consulting with gift and apparel stores, T.J. lives in Amite, a small Louisiana community, with her husband, Larry - the infamous "spider" on her shoulder. The mother she so proudly writes about in her titles, lives nearby. T.J., an only child, is the mother of two children, Billy (the fashion designer WILLIAM REID) and Laura Lea (a college student and assistant on the **FASHION ADVANTAGE**). She spends her free time writing, volunteering with local civic groups, shopping with best friend Betty, and doting over her only grandchild, Madeleine Jane. (And there's another little girl on the way!)

Reaching the half-century mark, T.J. realizes her childhood dream of fashion designs and novels in New York, hasn't quite come true, but it's certainly been close enough to make her life complete.

☆T.J. Reid's ORDER FORM

More Retail Details...Mother Forgot to Mention by T.J. Reid...$34.95_____

*What Mother Never Told Ya About Retail by T.J. Reid...$25.00_____

*52 Promotions: A Year's Worth of Profit! by T. J. Reid...$25.00_____

   **Both Books--Special $40.00 _____

Sell Yourself! 501 Ways to Get Them To Buy From You by Fred Berns.........................$22.00_____

1,001 Ways to Create Retail Excitement by Ed Falk...$20.00_____

Profit is Not A Four Letter Word ....$15.00_____

No Thanks, I'm Just Looking by Harry Friedman...$29.95_____

50 Powerful Ways to Keep Yours Customers...$10.00_____

1,001 Ways to Reward Your Employees by Bob Nelson...$12.00_____

T.J.'s Accessory Advantage video (48 minutes)...$20.00_____

Just Lookin' Coupons - Pack of 100...$10.00_____

☆*Fashion Advantage* Newsletter by T.J. Reid **(1 year - 10 issues)**...$129.00_____

To place an order call 800-221-8615, or mail payment to P. O. Box 977, Amite, Louisiana 70422.

Name:_____STORE:_____

Address:_____

City_____State_____Zip_____

Phone_____Fax_____

Credit Card_____Exp_____ or Check #_____

   Signature_____Dated_____

All Major Credit cards are accepted.
Shipping is $4.00 for one book or $8.00 for entire order. All shipments are made within 48 hours

800-221-8615/ Fax 504-748-8930/ E-Mail tj@tjreid.com